STORAGE &
SPACE-SAVING

HAMLYN PRACTICAL DIY GUIDES

STORAGE &
SPACE-SAVING

Jenny Plucknett & Peter Brooke-Ball

HAMLYN

ACKNOWLEDGMENTS

Copy editor:
Deborah Evans

❋

Technical consultant
Mike Trier

❋

Art editor:
Lee Griffiths

❋

Design:
Crucial Books

❋

Special photography:
Jon Bouchier

❋

Illustration:
Oxford Illustrators Limited

❋

Picture research:
Elizabeth Fowler

❋

Production controller:
Alyssum Ross

This edition published in 1990 by
The Hamlyn Publishing Group Limited
a division of the
Octopus Publishing Group
Michelin House
81 Fulham Road
London SW3 6RB

ISBN 0 600 564 681

Typeset by Flairplan Photo-typesetting
Produced by Mandarin Offset
Printed and bound in Hong Kong

CONTENTS

INTRODUCTION

For most of us, modern day living means fitting a surprising number of apparently essential belongings into a fairly small home. If you find it hard to imagine how you are going to store everything neatly away so it is easy to lay hands on when you need it and end up with an interior that is uncluttered and appears spacious, you are not alone.

This book aims to assist by first of all providing some suggestions for how you can find and utilize storage space in both obvious and unexpected parts of your home. It then shows with practical, helpful illustrations how to build storage units and space-saving furniture and how to make less used space more accessible. Finally it covers both general and specialist tools and materials needed for the work and provides useful hints on buying materials, caring for tools plus plenty of tips on how to ensure you get a professional result.

PART 1
FINDING THE SPACE

Start by taking a careful look at your own home, and see how you can apply some of the ideas shown here.

- Space in the home and how it can be rearranged.

- Methods of providing both display and hidden storage.

- A spacious effect and how it can be created.

- Dead space, like the understair cupboard or the roofspace, and how it can be turned to advantage.

- Room-by-room guide that provides answers to specific storage problems encountered in each room.

- Extra space outdoors and how it an be utilized for a porch, garage or garden shed.

PRACTICAL USE OF SPACE

Using the space you already have in the most practical way possible may involve some internal alteration such as dividing off a large bedroom to provide two smaller ones or knocking down a wall to give dining space within the kitchen.

Adding shelves and units to walls will give space

for storage that leaves the major area of floor uncluttered. Choosing the right internal fittings for cupboards can considerably improve storage facilities so that everything gets put away. Needless to say, being strict about keeping only the things you use allows more space for storing essentials!

Rearranging space

There are no rules about how the space in a home should be used, so do not be bound by convention but rather utilize the space in the best way to suit you and your lifestyle. For instance, a big kitchen with dining and living space and a small sitting room may suit a family better than the other way around.

It is worth considering how you would use extra rooms, if you had them. Then see if, by doubling up on the role of one room, you can include the extra requirements. A spare bedroom may also become a work or hobby room, a living room could also act as a periodic guest room.

Two rooms into one

By knocking down a wall you will gain a feeling of space but lose privacy. It is worth bearing in mind that you will also be removing walls that could be used for storage.

Interior walls, particularly plasterboard or lath and plaster on a stud frame, are comparatively simple to remove but sometimes even these can be load-bearing.

To decide if a wall is load-bearing look at the direction of the floor joists. If these, and those on the floor above, run at right angles to a wall then it is probably load-bearing. If the joists run parallel with the wall then this is unlikely, but the wall may support another partition wall in the upper storey.

If you are at all unsure about whether a wall is load-bearing or not contact the building inspector of your local council for advice – his approval is in any case necessary before you commence the work. If you intend removing a structural wall, or one bearing a partition above, a beam and piers will be needed to take the weight.

A rolled steel joist (RSJ) can be used to span an opening of any size but longer lengths are very heavy. Galvanized steel box beams are lighter and do not need special preparation before plastering (RSJs do). They are available up to 5.4m (17¾ft) long. Brick piers on properly constructed foundations are necessary to support whatever beam you use.

One room into two

If what you need is more rooms, then it is comparatively simple to install a partition wall to divide one room into two. There are rules governing

such things as window size to floor area, however, so check that the new rooms will comply with public health and building regulations before you start.

On a solid floor you can use lightweight building blocks which are easy to erect and have good sound insulation properties. These are finished with plasterboard panels on each side. On wood floors you can erect a simple framework of 50mm by 75mm (2in by 3in) rough sawn timber then nail plasterboard to

Below: In a small flat, a compact 'kitchen in a cupboard' leaves maximum space for eating and relaxing.

Efficient storage

There are two main ways of storing items: display storage for those belongings you want to show off and hidden storage for the less attractive equipment and the things you want to keep relatively dust free.

Display storage

Shelves provide ideal display storage and if you put them up or build them yourself they can be tailored to your needs.

Brackets screwed to the wall are best for individual shelves, while fixed battens create an unobtrusive base for alcove shelves. Alternatively, you can allow for some adjustment by using metal or wood uprights with regularly spaced holes into which you slot specially designed brackets. Shelves hung on slings anchored to the wall are another possibility for light objects.

The advantage of an adjustable system is not only that shelf positions can be altered at some future date when the use changes but also extra shelves can easily be added. See pages 36 – 43 for putting up shelves.

each side. The use of tape and joint filler will hide the joins between the boards. For detailed instructions on this sort of building work see the book *Building Projects* in this series.

Clearing space

You can make space by keeping only the things you use and so avoid cluttering storage areas with oddments that 'might come in useful sometime', but stay in the top of a cupboard, under the stairs or in the loft year after year.

When stored items go over a preset limit (say, six months without being used) get rid of them by selling through a local paper, a card in a shop window or a car boot sale. Real rubbish can be taken to the dump or removed by arrangement with the council refuse department (most will provide this service free of charge). Local charity shops may accept old clothes for re-sale.

Above: Fold back panels can hide a kitchen in a living room or open it up for use.

Right: A well planned wall of shelving allows just the right amount of space for everything.

Freestanding units

These allow you to take your storage system with you when you move. Modular systems, made to a standard height and depth, and consisting of boxes, some with the addition of doors or drawers, can be used to cover a whole wall from floor to ceiling or positioned in an alcove. You can also use them freestanding to divide off sections of a room, a study area in a bedroom or the loo in a bathroom for instance.

Ready-made systems are expensive, but you can make your own from veneered chipboard or blockboard, using plastic blocks to join the sections together and lay-on ready-made cupboard doors. The choice of board finishes and colours is wide and includes wood veneers, many plain colours and even leather look-alikes. You can cover edges with matching iron-on tape, or give them a more expensive finish with shaped timber moulding (the instructions on pages 42–43 give ideas for straight forward unit construction).

Hidden storage

Apart from providing an ideal spot for shelves, alcoves can be used very successfully for cupboards. You can make a deep cupboard to take a sideways hanging rail from plasterboard on a timber frame in much the same way as you would fit a stud wall. You can fix skirting and coving to the side and front and fit a room door or cupboard doors. The result is an unobtrusive yet usefully deep fitted cupboard (see page 50 for fitting instructions).

If you need a large cupboard the simplest way of providing one is to use a wardrobe kit with sliding doors that run on tracks at floor and ceiling level. You can fit end panels if the cupboard is to run only along part of a wall and add a ceiling batten if it is necessary to lower the ceiling height (see pages 52–54 for installation details).

Planning interior fitments

The great advantage of fitting your own storage system is that you can tailor it exactly to your own needs. Before ordering materials or internal units it is a good idea to assess the type and number of contents accurately, allowing for expansion, and then divide up the space to suit your particular needs.

> **TIP**
> Wall storage can provide additional heat insulation if placed on an outside wall, and sound insulation on a party wall. Books are especially effective for both.

Left: *Freestanding units can easily be reorganised when required and will even move with you.*

A SENSE OF SPACE

Colour schemes, furnishings, furniture and its arrangement all contribute to a feeling of spaciousness or clutter. A light interior gives an impression of space and reflective surfaces, especially mirrors, can increase the apparent size of a room. All these factors can be used to trick the eye.

Colour choice

Light colours appear to recede, dark ones to advance, so a room painted in pale tones will seem much more spacious than the same room decorated in deep colours. Large, bold patterns will also appear to shrink space, while plain colours or small, muted designs create the opposite effect.

Texture too can play its part in expanding an area. Shiny surfaces such as mirrors reflect and give an impression of space. Therefore a small choice, like painting a room in silk finish rather than matt emulsion, can contribute to how large a room appears. Use a light colour to make a ceiling recede, a deeper colour if you want to lower the apparent height of walls and ceiling.

Light-coloured flooring will, again, make a room appear larger and if you use the same pale colour throughout a small house or flat, rather than breaking up the space with a patchwork of tints, the difference will be considerable. If you enclose the space with a deep colour skirting, you will shrink it again.

Horizontal lines increase width, vertical lines increase depth in a room just as they do in the clothes we wear, so the look of a long, narrow room can be improved by vinyl tiles or a carpet with lines running across it, or rows of shelves at one end. Full length curtains on the end wall or those with vertical stripes make the room appear narrower.

Diagonal lines can also contribute to a feeling of spaciousness.

Furniture choice

Low furniture, which the eye travels over, helps to make a room appear larger and, of course, the use of light colours both for wood and furnishings helps too. Match furniture colour to flooring and the furniture will appear less obvious. A number of small items of furniture dotted around a room will give a cluttered look that is lost when all the necessary bits and pieces are placed along one wall.

Below: *Light colours for walls and flooring and low, light furniture help to create a feeling of space.*

Unit furniture that can be arranged to form an L or U shape against walls also provides a less cluttered look than the standard sofa and two chairs. Glass-topped tables, because you can see through them and because of the shiny, reflective texture, are another good choice.

Use of mirrors

Clever use of mirrors is one of the best ways of creating a sense of space. A wall of mirrors can double a room's apparent size and mirrored doors on a fitted wardrobe will have the same effect. When buying large pieces of mirror, remember to check that you can manoeuvre them into position when you get them home.

Apart from fixing through pre-drilled holes with screws, large pieces of mirror will need to rest on a platform such as a skirting edge or worktop which will take the weight. J-section aluminium strip is a good alternative.

A mirror can only reflect what is opposite or adjacent to it, and if this is a plain wall little is gained. So it is a good idea, before you put up a mirror, to check the reflection with a smaller hand-held mirror first, then adjust the position if necessary. A mirror will draw light into the room if it is placed to reflect a window, or small mirror tiles can be used on the window's inner reveals to increase light. Mirror tiles are a simple way to create a wall of mirror, but they must be fitted to a level surface.

Adding light

Light is another space-creating factor. In dark areas such as halls it is therefore worth considering replacing panels or whole doors with glazed sections. When replacing wood panels with glass use toughened or laminated safety glass and hold the glass in place with beading.

Above: *Track lighting above a mirror can increase the light in the room.*

Below: *A narrow hall can appear twice as wide by fixing mirror along one wall.*

SAFETY POINT
If you use mirrors to create an illusion of extra space, it is important to place plants or furniture in such a way that people will not try to walk through them.

QUICK TIP
Use mirror tiles to provide the impression of an extra window or doorway by surrounding a rectangle of tiles with architrave. You can even add 'glazing bars' for a realistic effect. Mirror tiles need to be fixed to a totally flat surface or the result will be a misshapen image, so if the wall is not flat use a piece of blockboard fixed to battens on the wall as a base.

EXTRA SPACE

Some parts of most homes, because they are inaccessible, like the loft space, or awkwardly shaped, like the understairs cupboard, become disorganized dumping grounds. These, together with other smaller areas such as fireplaces, corners and even doors, can be transformed into easy-to-use storage space, often with only small adjustments.

Adding a porch, a conservatory or a garden shed can also provide extra space to take the stress off the home's interior.

Doors and doorways

Cupboard and room doors provide space for easy-to-get-at narrow storage. Choose from metal racks and plastic shelves for the kitchen, hanging pocketed holdalls for shoes, small toys, socks or tights for the bedroom.

A small towel rail will probably fit on the back of the bathroom door, or hang a pocketed holdall to take bathroom paraphernalia such as shampoo, talc, toothbrushes and paste.

A towel rail on the inside of a bedroom cupboard door can take jeans, ties or belts. Large hooks fixed on the back of the cloakroom door could hold mops, brooms or a lightweight stepladder. Check hinges and screws are adequate to take the weight of larger items. Hollow doors are unsuitable for heavy objects.

Sometimes simple changes to the way a door opens can provide easier access or make the surrounding space much more accessible. Installing a sliding door could be the answer in a confined space. Turning a door round to open on the opposite side could allow you to place furniture in a room in a much more practical position (see pages 55–58 for turning a door round; fitting a sliding door is dealt with in the instructions for installing a fitted wardrobe on pages 52–54).

Fireplaces

If fireplaces are unused, and those in bedrooms and kitchens nearly always are, then their removal will leave a space that can either be extended or used as it is for storage (see page 65 for further advice).

Alternative uses

- Build in a storage unit that exactly fits the space.
- Use it for wine storage.

- Increase the height of the opening (take professional advice) and fit a fridge/freezer or stacked fridge and freezer in the space.
- Place a chest of drawers and mirror in the space.
- Fit with shelves for a display of plants, shells, glassware or any other collection.
- Add shelves and doors to provide a larder cupboard.

If space is very tight then removing a complete chimney may just provide the necessary extra centimetres. This is not an easy job, however, as chimneys are nearly always an integral part of the house and, sometimes, the house next door too. This means that steps must be taken to ensure that this part of the house remains structurally stable. Obtain professional advice before you start.

Cupboards and corners

A deep cupboard or unused passage space may provide the necessary room for installing a shower – you will need floorspace of 90cm by 90cm (3ft by 3ft), height of 2m (6½ft) and access space of about 75cm (30in).

Provided the cold water cistern in the loft is 1.2m (4ft) above the shower outlet you can install a mixer

Above: A fireplace is used for easily accessible wine storage in this dining room.

shower with separate controls for water flow and temperature. Otherwise you will need to use an instantaneous shower, usually electric, where in most cases water flow and temperature are related, so the greater the flow the lower the temperature will be.

You can build partition sides and tile them or install a cubicle. Corner units are now also available. See *Plumbing and Central Heating,* in this series, for instructions on how to install a shower.

A long, narrow understairs cupboard usually ends up with floor space packed so that items stored at the far end can only be reached by removing everything else first. By removing side panelling, the space becomes shallow and wide, rather than long and narrow, making it much more efficient for storage. Alternatively, in an open plan living room or small hall, this can become part of the room itself.

Using the roof space

By adding flooring and providing easy access by means of a retractable loft ladder the roof space becomes a large, easy to use storage area that will take almost everything you might want to keep (see pages 60–61 for installation information).

If the roof area is high enough you may be able to transform it into extra living space by inserting dormer windows and a fixed staircase. Discuss this initially with your local council's Building Control Office as building regulations differ depending on such things as the age of the house and the number of floors. The capacity of the roof joists also needs to be taken into account as these may need strengthening (see page 59 for more information).

Adding a porch

A porch is especially valuable where the front door opens directly on to a living room. Whether this be the case or not, a porch provides insulation and, if large enough, space for boots, umbrellas and outer clothes.

Porch kits are available, usually comprising a simple timber frame structure and fully glazed or half glazed wall and door units, but it is not difficult to put a porch together using off-the-shelf wall units and vestibule frames with your choice of windows and ready-prepared corner posts to join the frames together. A roof sloping towards the front can be made from roof decking and roofing felt. You will need to lay a solid foundation incorporating a damp proof membrane which does not come above the damp course of the house.

If a porch is not more than 2sq m (2½ sq yd) in floor area and 3m (10ft) high and is not within 2m (6½ft) of your roadside boundary it does not normally require planning permission unless you live in a conservation area or a listed building. Check with your local Planning Office if you are unsure.

Putting up a shed

A garden shed 2m by 1½m (6½ft by 5ft) should provide adequate space for storing paint, materials and DIY equipment and tools, plus a fold-away workbench as well as gardening paraphernalia. Pick a site that is dry and level and, if you want to include lighting and power points, not too far from the house. If you cannot avoid placing it in view of the house you can train evergreen climbers over it to soften the hard lines.

Metal and concrete-panel sheds are available as well as the more common timber ones. Softwood sheds may need treating with preservative; others will have already been pressure impregnated and this is the longer-lasting alternative. Hardwoods are naturally durable.

Below: A glazed-in entrance porch helps retain heat in the rest of the house.

HALLS, STAIRS AND LANDINGS

Often narrow and awkwardly shaped, halls, stairs and landings can usually take only a minimum of furniture. At first sight finding space for storage appears practically impossible, but walls will provide room for a wall-hung telephone and noticeboard and there is often just enough width for a shallow cupboard for outdoor clothing or for narrow shelves. Walls and windows can contribute by providing space for decorative displays. Alterations to the understair cupboard can often considerably increase its storage potential or turn it into a useful cloakroom, shower space or laundry area. By removing side panelling the hall can be enlarged, providing room for a telephoning area or space for hanging outdoor clothes out of the passageway.

Left: *A hall alcove provides useful space for an office with desk and telephone.*

Right: *A wall-mounted phone is useful when there is no room for a table.*

Long, narrow halls

In many cases halls are so narrow that using space at the sides for standard width shelves or a shallow cupboard cuts down on essential passage space and therefore is not practical.

A wall-hung telephone means that a table is not necessary. Fix a noticeboard nearby if you want callers' messages passed on but make sure pad and pencil are included, along with a calendar and any family reminders. A couple of small wire bicycle baskets could be fixed with cup hooks to the wall below to hold mail. Alternatively, place the telephone and noticeboard above the radiator – which takes up space, along a wall anyway – and add a single shelf on brackets. If you let it, this will soon become very popular with the family cat!

A simple made-to-measure noticeboard can be made from cork wall tiles stuck to a sheet of hardboard. Alternatively, use 6mm (¼in) medium density fibreboard as the backing, cut larger than the tiles to accommodate a timber moulding frame with mitred corners. Make it large enough and one cork tile could be replaced by mirror tiles.

A coat rack that screws to the wall is very simple to make. A piece of timber 20mm (¾in) thick and 100–150mm (4–6in) wide is a good size for the base. Cut it to a length to suit its position and the number of items you want to be able to hang. Use double brass or chrome hooks or door knobs in a variety of sizes (door knobs are not suitable if you want to hang coats from the back loop but are fine for use with coathangers). Space hooks at least 200mm (8in) apart, (500mm (20in) if you intend to use with coat hangers). Measure, mark, then screw the hooks or knobs in position on the base. Finally, screw the rack in place on the wall. You could also include plastic-coated spring clips to take walking sticks and umbrellas.

End walls

It may be possible to use the wall surrounding a door at the end of a hall for narrow shelves. Based on the instructions on page 42, build a box shelving system to cover the complete wall, leaving a door-sized space in the centre.

QUICK TIP

To reflect light and provide a feeling of spaciousness glue mirror mosaic tiles on their fabric backing to the panels of traditional doors or all over a flush door.

Hall and landing windows

Glass shelves, placed at intervals across a window, provide space to display plants or a collection of glass or china. If you want to be able to change shelf positions use thin strip aluminium shelving supports screwed to the frame recess. For safety it is important to use lipped brackets that stop the glass from slipping, plus 6mm (¼in) glass with polished edges.

Shallow cupboards

Use an alcove to create a shallow cupboard with tall, narrow louvre or panelled doors (see pages 50–51). Alternatively, fit a floor to ceiling cupboard with sliding doors (see pages 52–54).

If you want to use the cupboard to store outdoor clothing it will need to be a minimum of 30cm (12in) deep. Fit it with hooks (see page 93) or a coat rack or, if you have the width, fit a pull-out clothes rail that runs from front to back.

A rack for boots and shoes can be fitted into the base using three lengths of small dowel fixed into triangular shaped blocks of timber at each end to form a right-angled triangle so that the top rail holds the heels in position. Alternatively, use short lengths of thicker dowel slotted into a wooden backplate on which shoes can hang.

If you have the wall space for a large cupboard one section could be turned into a tool storage area. Cut out a board base and arrange tools on it, then fit it with spring clips and hooks where required. When it is screwed in place on the back wall you could add one or two narrow shelves for jam jars to hold nails and screws. Screw the lids of more jam jars to the underside of the shelf to provide twice the storage space.

On the landing a similar cupboard could be fitted with shelves to take linen and small items of clothing.

> **QUICK TIP**
>
> There is always room for a key rack. You could make your own by cutting out a simple house or family pet shape with a jig or fret saw from timber or painted board. Then screw a series of brass cup hooks to it to hold the keys. It is wise to place this well out of the reach of small children and away from windows.

Below: A shelf across the corner of the stairs shows off plants, lit from above.

Stair corners

Where stairs make a quarter or half turn there may be room for a corner cupboard (see page 46). Triangular wall shelves will take up less space and could be fixed above head height and used to display favourite ornaments. Alternatively, you could use two or three hanging baskets on brackets screwed to the wall at different heights for a plant display. In most cases you will need to choose shade-loving varieties like creeping fig or maidenhair fern if they are to flourish.

Large halls or landings

If you are lucky enough to have a large hall or landing then you have the opportunity to use part of the space for a dining area, study or sewing room. In a confined spot fit a flap down table (see page 48) and use fold-up chairs that can be hung on hooks on the wall when not in use.

Below: Space on a landing has been put to use here as a study and eating area.

CONVERTING THE UNDERSTAIR SPACE

Staircase structure

What you can do with the space under your staircase depends on its structure. Most staircases are supported by at least one adjacent wall on one side and by what is known as a string (running diagonally from one floor to the next) on the other. These cannot be removed unless you provide an alternative support and so are best incorporated within any scheme. Newel posts are fitted at either end of the string, and at the top of the flight they are also fixed to the joists either by housing or mortise and tenon joints.

Straight run staircase This has a triangular space below and is normally installed against a load-bearing wall with a full height newel supporting its outer edge. The alternative to this is a straight run staircase with a wall on each side, in which case each wall bears the staircase weight and this makes it very difficult to open up the underneath space from the side.

Quarter-turn staircase This has a few steps at the top or the bottom fixed at right angles to the rest. It is also installed against a load-bearing wall with a newel post supporting the top of the string at the turn.

Half-turn staircase This is normally constructed in a similar way to a quarter-turn one, with the small lower landing being supported by a joist and the upper landing by timbers (bearers) built into the wall adjacent to the staircase.

In a half-turn or upper level quarter-turn staircase a cloakroom has often been fitted into the high level space beneath the stairs by the original builder.

Above: *Opening up the understair space allows room for outdoor clothes storage.*

Left: *Shelves under a staircase keep clutter out of the living room.*

Normally, newel posts are mainly decorative, acting as support for banisters. At turns, they also support strings. In some constructions, they are built from floor to ceiling, and cannot be removed. Intermittent newels may carry part of the weight of the stairs and are better not removed.

Space where you can stand upright

This is obviously the most useful understair area. You will need a height of 2m (6½ft) plus floor space of just under 1m × 1m (3¼ft × 3¼ft) to install a shower. A lavatory will fit into a space 700mm × 1m (2¼ft × 3¼ft) but some extra width or length will be needed for a basin. If space is tight, use either a corner or specially shallow basin that is sunk into the wall.

Where surrounding space is limited use two tall, narrow cupboard doors rather than a wider room door.

A washing machine and stacked tumble dryer will need less height, around 1.5m (5ft) and, depending on make, approximately 700mm by 700mm (2¼ft × 2¼ft) floor space.

How easy and inexpensive new plumbing will be will depend on how close this area is to existing plumbing in the kitchen and bathroom. For more information on plumbing see *Plumbing and Central Heating*, also in this series. If you need to move the gas or electricity meters you must consult the respective Boards.

Opening up from the side

If you remove partitions at the side of the stairs this area, depending on size, can be incorporated with the adjoining space to be used as a tiny study, sewing area or telephone space, or fitted with racks for outdoor clothes storage. It can also be used much more efficiently for storage space.

If the staircase is positioned in an open plan living room the space underneath can be used like an alcove and fitted from floor to ceiling with a shelving system.

LIVING ROOMS

Comfortable seating is often bulky and needs careful arranging if it is not to overpower the room. Storage becomes streamlined if it is placed along one wall instead of being dotted around the room. Special wall brackets mean loudspeakers or TV can be placed in the best possible position for good acoustics and viewing yet be out of the way.

Dining space can be divided off with shelving or double up as a work and study area and, with some forethought, the room can be organized so that it can quickly be turned into a bedroom for overnight guests.

Making a room plan

After you have renovated a room – or moved into a new home – it is a good idea to draw out a floor plan to scale on graph paper, the larger the better, to find the furniture arrangement that is going to make the best use of the available space. Mark on it the positions of sockets and radiators. Measure each item of furniture you want to include and cut out shapes from coloured paper to the same scale. Write on them what they are and then move them about on the plan until you are happy with the arrangement.

Estimate your storage requirements in a similar way so you can calculate the number of shelves or cupboards you will need, plus the depths and the heights required. Allow extra space for additions – a designer, when planning storage, usually allows for double the present required space!

Deciding on a seating arrangement

Where and how sofas and chairs are positioned will depend mainly on the shape of the room, the position of any fireplace, radiators and windows and whether you want to use the room for regular or irregular meals as well.

How many people will you want to seat most of the time? Can you bring chairs from elsewhere in the house for extra visitors? If not, you could consider providing fold-up director chairs that can be stored in the understair cupboard and do double duty for meals outdoors in the summer.

Practical and space-saving seating plans

1 Two sofas placed in an L arrangement will fit neatly against adjacent walls, perhaps sited to face the fireplace one way and windows the other.
2 In an especially small room, unit seating arranged around two or three walls allows you to seat the greatest number of people.
3 Two sofas placed opposite each other are best for conversation. If one divides the room it will be less obtrusive if it is low-backed.

Storage

Alcoves provide an ideal spot for shelves and the range of available systems and designs make it possible to suit any style of house and furnishings.

In an old house it looks good if shelving matches other timber in the room. Moulding designs can be matched too – for instance, the timber moulding used for the skirting edge can be repeated in the shelf supports, or screwed to the sides and back of the alcove and mitred at the corners.

To complement modern surroundings an adjustable system of brightly coloured metal uprights and brackets could be used, or, if you have modern pine furniture, match it with solid-looking pine battens with equally spaced holes drilled in them to take dowel studs as shelf supports. See pages 35–41 for putting up shelves.

If you are a great collector of books, records and tapes and bits and pieces you may want to use a complete wall for their display. You could use one of the systems mentioned above and vary the width of brackets and shelves to suit the items to be stored. Alternatively, build in a boxed system from melamine finished or veneered chipboard or blockboard, fixing the boxes together with plastic jointing blocks. It is fairly simple to include cup-

Above: *The alcoves beside a fireplace are ideal for a built-in shelving system.*

boards too if you plan the size of the sections for hidden storage to match up with available cupboard doors. See page 42 for construction.

Room dividers

The same boxed storage system can be used to build a divider between sitting and eating areas. (You could also make one to the height and depth of the sofa arm, so that placed against it the unit will form a convenient table surface as well as providing space for books, magazines and newspapers.)

You can make a very simple see-through division from rigid garden trellis. Screw battens to the wall, ceiling and a section of the floor at each side, then fix trellis panels to these to form a large squared-off arch. Where you need to join sections, use battens twice the width of the trellis frame. Butt up the sections to be joined and screw each to the batten. Paint to match the room scheme. Climbing plants grown in troughs at the base can weave their way upwards over the trellis.

Housing video, TV and stereo

Storing TV and video on a trolley makes manoeuvring them into the right viewing position easy. Another alternative is to fit a TV bracket that allows the same adaptability but leaves floor space free. Similar brackets designed to hold small stereo speakers pivot so that the speaker can be angled accurately for the best possible sound reception. Both are simple to fix – see page 44.

Displaying plants

Plants nearly always look best when grouped rather than displayed individually. A single shelf above the radiator and in front of a window is an ideal spot. Line up the plants in a trough. Very few plants enjoy the dry heat provided by a radiator and most will only thrive in high humidity so place the pots on a bed of damp shingle or surround them with peat.

Dining area

Choosing the best dining table will depend on the shape of the space available. Extra diners can usually be accommodated at a round table and this is the most sociable shape. Drop leaf or extending tables provide versatility but you can also cut your own larger spare top from blockboard, store it away and place it on top of your normal table, covered with a cloth, for occasions when there are extra visitors. If space is very tight make a fold-down table that fixes to the wall. Allow a 90cm (3ft) space for pulling back a chair.

Overnight guests

If you do not have a spare bedroom it makes sense to plan the living-room furniture and its arrangement around accommodating occasional overnight guests. This means choosing a sofa bed (check how comfortable it is in both positions before buying) and providing a bedside table plus lighting that can be switched on and off from the bed. Allocate some storage space for bedding during the day.

QUICK TIP

A very simple way of putting together your own dining table is to use a flush door as the table top and simply place it on two trestles. If you choose folding trestles the whole thing can be stored away in a narrow space when not required.

Above: *A clever system of sliding shelves conceals a fold-down bed.*

Above: *The bed in position.*

KITCHENS

More equipment is stored in the kitchen, in an often restricted space, than anywhere else in the house, Good, easy-to-reach storage facilities are essential and can make all the difference to a task's ease and enjoyment.

Most people live with a kitchen planned and fitted by someone else whose lifestyle and needs were probably not the same as theirs. In spite of this, simple improvements can be made by fitting out cupboard interiors with wire racks and extra

shelves. Further storage can be provided by filling wall space with shelves and using racks and rails behind the work surface. The sensible positioning of stored supplies and equipment also helps considerably towards a kitchen's smooth running.

For those of you who are putting in a new kitchen here are some ideas for drawing up a plan of a kitchen that will be tailor-made to suit you. There are tips on fitting units and services and advice on what jobs are better done by the experts.

Efficient storage

If items are not easily accessible the chances are that they will be left out after use to clutter whatever working space there is – and if this area has to be cleared every time meals are to be prepared no one is going to enjoy working in the kitchen.

You will use space most efficiently if you bear the following points in mind:

1 The most frequently used items need storing in the most accessible space.

2 If equipment utensils and stores are placed at the position in the kitchen where they are first to be used, time and effort will be cut down.

3 Adding racks and extra shelves to cupboard interiors will cut down on the need to stack contents. Stacking leads to accidents as well as physical wear and tear through excess bending, stretching and lifting.

Items in frequent use

Equipment and utensils which are needed a number of times each day should be especially accessible. The area most easy to reach is that between hip and shoulder height and this is often the space left free in fitted kitchens. Where there is available space at this height it is a good idea to utilize it by erecting shelves and putting up grid system racks and metal rails.

Professionally planned storage

In a commercial kitchen the area is divided into work stations – pastry making, sauce making, vegetable

Above: Whatever the shape, start to plan a kitchen with the most used spot, which is the preparation area between the hob and sink.

and salad preparation and so on. Within the station all the equipment and food for that particular job is stored so that it is not necessary to go from one side of the kitchen to the other to collect items.

This efficient system can be of benefit to the home cook too. All that is probably needed is some simple reorganization as follows:

Cooking area (Next to the hob and possibly, but not essentially, next to the oven.) Store cooking utensils, any pans that go straight to the cooker (those that are first filled with water are stored by the sink) plus pan lids, cooking tools, foil, anything that goes straight into the pot (herbs, oil, spices, canned foods like tomatoes and baked beans, rice and pasta).

Preparation centre (Preferably between hob or cooker and sink.) Tools for mixing and baking, bowls, measuring jug, scales, cutting boards, casseroles, baking supplies and all foods mixed or prepared before use.

Sink area Any equipment first filled with water plus utensils like colanders and strainers, rubbish bin and liners, foods that need water adding, cleaning materials.

Snack making and serving area (Close to the eating area, next to microwave and kettle and close to the fridge.) Coffee and tea making ingredients, mugs, breadboard and knife, toaster, heated tray, dishes, glassware, cutlery, table linen, food served at table.

Extra fitments

These can go a long way towards making your storage space more accessible. The range shown below is not just available as an extra with new units but can be fitted to most standard-size kitchen units as well.

Extra shelves These remove the necessity for stacking the contents of cupboards. You can buy studs to hold shelves and slot them into holes drilled in the cupboard sides at regular intervals or you can use metal or plastic strip. Melamine faced chipboard 20mm (¾in) thick is adequate

Left: A rack that stores plates vertically is decorative and easy to use.

Below, left and right: The use of pull out shelves or drawers means contents are easy to see and to reach.

for most stored equipment.

Wire racks Plate racks allow you to store saucers and plates vertically rather than horizontally, making them much easier to remove and replace. Shallow back-of-door racks provide added storage space for small items such as spices, packets, tubes and small tins or cleaning materials.

Plinth storage Do not waste floor level space – tools can be stored in shallow trays here, or you can use the space for folding steps that can be quickly retrieved and unfolded to provide safe access to high-level cupboards. A bracket is available with steps that allows them to be swung

under the plinth.

Fold-away surfaces Ideal for limited space are ironing boards and tables that fold into two or three sections and then slide to fit inside the top and back of a cupboard when not in use. Mixer and food processor shelves hold equipment in the cupboard then lift to fit flush with the worktop for use. All these come with full fitting instructions.

Drawers These are now considered one of the most practical forms of storage. There is less stooping involved in removing the contents, which are easy to see and reach. Some unit ranges consist only of drawers of varying widths and depths. Wire baskets that pull out on runners are a good alternative, and you can buy them both shallow and deep enough to take pans. Four shallow baskets can replace shelves in a floor unit, while the deeper baskets fit on to a pair of shelves with runners.

Waste bins Bins can be fitted that swing out when the unit door is opened, leaving the lid behind. The newest bin is fitted into the worktop, where a hole is cut in the same way as for an inset sink or hob. The rim and lid fit over this and a bin liner is anchored by the rim and removed when full from the cupboard below.

Narrow spaces You can use a space between floor units for a telescopic towel rail. Two- and three-arm rails are available. Attach the fixing plate to the back wall or to the underside of the work surface.

Turning a problem to advantage

In a small kitchen every centimetre of space has to work for you. Here are some suggestions for overcoming common problems and at the same time giving the room your own individual touch:

Limited width in a narrow passage kitchen Where there is only space for units and working surface along one side of the kitchen consider putting up shallow shelves that run from floor to ceiling along the opposite wall. This form of storage, suitable for dried foods as well as utensils and china and glass, is immensely practical as everything can be easily seen – there is just no room for one item to be hidden from view behind another. If you do not want everything to be always on show fix roller blinds to the ceiling to drop down in front of the shelves. These can be left up when work is in progress, then lowered afterwards.

Hard-to-reach corners Ideal in this situation are revolving wire or plastic tray carousels which swing out towards you, providing easy access to those items stored at the back. In quarter-turn carousels the baskets are fitted to the door jamb and have revolving hinge fittings. Half-turn trays fit on to a tube, as do three-quarter corner carousel trays. When planning a new kitchen, consider placing the cooker or sink at an angle across the corner; this position provides extra working space around the fitment and space for utensils at the back.

Lack of eating space A rectangular or semi-circular drop-down table that fits snug against the wall when not in use could provide the answer (see page 48 for construction). Add fold-up chairs that can be hung on hooks on the wall on either side. If no wall space is available you could consider a table that slides back into a unit when not in use. Both would also provide extra workspace.

Cluttered worktops

This usually means that equipment and utensils are difficult to put away – see the previous pages for some answers to this problem. Take advantage of the space between worktop and wall units to fit shallow shelves for smaller equipment and hanging rails and racks for utensils. A 200mm (8in) deep shelf can take much of the equipment otherwise left at the back of the work surface and release space below for stores needed temporarily during food preparation. It is only the front two-thirds of the worktop that is usually required for the actual preparation.

When drilling into ceramic tiles for a screw fixing, stick adhesive tape over the position of the hole before you begin to stop the drill bit from slipping.

Old-fashioned units

It is simple to give old units a new look by replacing the cupboard doors

Above: Shallow shelves provide one of the most efficient forms of kitchen storage.

Above left: *A breakfast bar and stools provide eating space in a small kitchen.*
Above right: *A table that slides out of a unit also provides extra eating space.*
Left: *Fold up chairs can be stored in a narrow space or even hung from the wall.*
Right: *Racks and shelves maximise storage; rails hold cooking utensils.*

and drawer fronts with standard size lay-on doors hung with concealed lay-on cabinet hinges (see page 93). These make aligning doors much easier than it used to be. There is also a wide range of handles to choose from.

Planning a new kitchen

A small kitchen, where everything is stored close to hand, is the most practical to work in and even in a large area success relies on the space being broken down into smaller sections.

Large kitchens, used for relaxing as well as preparing food and eating, have become very popular in the last decade. In fact the kitchen is fast taking over from the living room as the place where friends as well as family naturally congregate.

Often the only way to find the space needed for this multi-use area is to incorporate an adjoining room within the scheme. See page 8 for information on recognizing and removing load-bearing walls.

Lifestyle

In many homes now the cooking is no longer done by one person alone, but approached as a joint task, particularly where both members of a couple are working. With the introduction of microwave cookers many younger members of a family now make their own snacks and quite often want to do so at the same time as an evening meal is being prepared.

This has resulted in a totally new look at kitchen planning, which invariably used to be based on a working triangle. Sink, cooker and refrigerator were placed on two or three separate walls but as close to each other as possible to create a working area that formed a triangle between the three. This is fine if only one person does the cooking, but it causes chaos when two or three people are trying to prepare food at the same time.

Layouts for working area

Depending on how many people will work in the kitchen, bear the following points in mind:

The multi-cook kitchen In this case you need to plan the kitchen with a main prepartion area close to sink and hob or cooker and a secondary space where hot drinks and snacks can be made. This section should include the kettle, toaster and microwave, and perhaps also the oven. The refrigerator and food will need to be accessible from each.

The one-cook kitchen The food preparation area is the centre of most work in the kitchen so the position of this is the first thing to be decided upon. Then equipment; hob, sink, refrigerator and larder are planned around and as close to it as possible. Storage space is planned around each working area (see work stations listed under Professionally planned storage, pages 20–21).

A backward look

Kitchen designers are realizing that some of the contents of the traditional kitchen are especially practical for use today. These are some of the oldies to bear in mind when planning your kitchen.

The dresser Uses that valuable storage space between hip and shoulder again. China and cookware stored on shelves is immediately apparent and much easier to reach than that hidden away in floor level or high cupboards.

The larder A floor-to-ceiling ventilated step-in larder with shelves of varying heights and depths on three sides allows more storage in a given space than wall and floor units, so it is the most valuable way of storing foodstuffs in a small kitchen.

The kitchen table A centrally positioned table can be used to divide off different working areas of the kitchen and is the ideal height for many jobs like pastry making and chopping. It also provides an area where visitors can make themselves comfortable.

Planning check list

Before a kitchen is planned on paper it is important to work out how you want to use it, so the result is designed to suit your personal lifestyle. A kitchen designer would start by asking a number of questions, listed below, so note down the answers and use them yourself when making your own plan. It is a mistake to tackle it the other way around and start by working out what you can fit into the space you have. The list highlights priorities.

1 What do you want to use the kitchen for; cooking, eating, laundry, ironing, relaxing, hobbies, home office?

2 How many people (and pets) will use the kitchen?

3 What appliances do you require – one oven or two, hob, microwave, refrigerator, freezer, dishwasher, washing machine, tumble dryer? List them and note which need special plumbing or ventilation.

4 How much storage space do you need? Work this out from present storage and add one third to one half on top. Do not forget space and facilities for rubbish.

5 How many electric outlets will you need? Check your plan when finalizing to see that lighting is adequate for all surfaces.

6 Have you anywhere else that laundry equipment could go – the cloakroom or bathroom, for instance?

7 Have you made a note of what is wrong with your present kitchen?

Drawing up your design

If you buy self-assembly units you will probably find that the stockist will offer assistance with the design. Where help is not available use large grid paper for ease and draw on to it the outline of your kitchen, noting doors and which way they open, windows, and any fixed items – radiator, boiler, gas pipes, plumbing (all these can be moved, see below, but if you need to call in an expert the cost increases). Include windowsill height, ceiling and door heights and so on.

Cut out shapes of units and equipment to the same scale, mark them with what they are and place those

Left: *A shallow floor to ceiling cupboard used for food storage must be ventilated.*

that need specific positioning first – but consult your check list. If the kitchen is the main route to the garden, take care over positioning the cooker. Carefully double check your final plan. Using this, make up the list of materials you will need.

PLAN OF WORK

Electrics

If you are replacing an old kitchen with a new one you will probably need more electrical outlets. Assuming you have a ring main you can add one extra socket outlet to each existing one by means of a spur. If this will not give you enough outlets a special kitchen circuit will be necessary and in this case it is better to call in a qualified electrician.

Gas

The flexible hose fitted to most modern cookers allows you about 30cm (12in) leeway on either side of your present cooker position. Running new gas pipes to alter the position is not difficult. All gas connections must be made and checked by a registered gas installer.

It is vital to turn the gas off at the mains and ventilate the room thoroughly while you are working. Use pre-soldered capillary fittings and work with scrupulous cleanliness.

You will need 15mm (½in) copper tubing to carry the gas and a good flux to ensure a good joint, plus a small blow lamp to apply the heat to the pre-soldered fittings. Check joins with a solution of detergent when you first turn the gas back on and before lighting the appliance. Smear it over joints: bubbles will appear if there is a leak. When you do light the appliance let the gas escape for a few seconds before you ignite it.

If you are having any plumbing done the fitter will include gas work at very little extra charge.

Plumbing

Plumbing is simple if you do not want to move the sink position and can put the dishwasher and washing machine on either side. You can buy undersink traps with built-in connectors to take the waste water from the machines. The hoses push on.

If you want to move the sink it should be possible to place it anywhere on an outside wall, or on an internal wall within about 1m (3ft) of an outside wall, but the shorter the run of waste water pipe the less chance there is of a blockage.

Floor

Use a long spirit level to check the floor level. A difference of 10mm (⅓in) across the floor is normal. At this point assemble the units, put them in position without fixing and lay the worktop in place. If an egg laid on the worktop stays in place the floor is level enough, if it rolls the units or floor will need adjustment. A solid floor can be rescreeded or the units and plinths can be trimmed to fit. These are skilled jobs and it is better to call in an expert to do the work.

Walls

Lay a strip of metal along the face of the wall. Check where it touches the wall and where it does not. Minor variations do not matter but if they are more than 20mm (¾in) fitting the worktop will be a problem. Choosing a worktop with an upstand at the back that you can fill behind with a silicone bathroom sealant is one way of getting around variations but if the problem is severe the worktop will need to be scribed and planed to fit. The skills of a professional joiner are required for this.

Joins in worktops are possible using aluminium strip but a professionally made joint looks far better. Most suppliers will do this for you but when supplying measurements you need to take into account any variation in the two adjoining walls to get an accurate fit.

Fitting units

Fit a wooden batten to the wall level with the top of the units. This gives extra room for plumbing and cuts out the need for access slots in the sides and backs of the units. Do not screw down the batten so hard that it follows bumps and hollows.

Place the floor units in position, check the plumbing and electrics line up, then use a jig or sharp pad saw to cut holes in the back where necessary for services to pass through.

Fix the units to each other through the sides. Check that the backs fit correctly and slide them down in position. Run glue along the sides of the panels first for stronger assembly.

Using metal right-angled brackets, fix the units to the battens.

Offer up the worktop to check the fit against the wall. If necessary hack away the plaster then repair the wall when the worktop is in position using exterior filler.

Screw up through the units into the worktop to fix it. Using a jigsaw, cut holes for the sink and hob in the worktop and fit and fix these in place. Check that they work.

Add doors and drawers to the base units and adjust the hinges so that the doors hang level.

Assemble the wall units and, using a spirit level, hang these.

Tile above the worktop if required. It is important for hygiene reasons to use an epoxy grout. Fit plinths, cornices and concealed lighting.

TIPS
- Save worktop space by using special purpose brackets to hang a microwave on the wall.
- A wall telephone with noticeboard and shelf nearby plus tall stool will provide a useful planning and organization area.
- Use an internal windowsill to house a window box full of herbs, making a dash into the garden in the rain unnecessary. Fast-growing species like mint and lemon balm need to be contained in pots sunk into the compost or they will soon take over.

BEDROOMS

In most modern homes bedrooms are small, allowing space for little except the bed and clothes storage. Here, more than anywhere else, bare walls and all available nooks and crannies need to be utilized. Alcoves, corners, fireplaces, even under the bed are all spots that can be turned into storage space. A large or spare bedroom can provide room for additional activities other than sleeping and a tiny spare room or box room, too small for a bed, could become a walk-in closet where all the family's clothes can be stored to take the strain off bedroom space.

Using walls

A fitted wardrobe, because it spans the space between floor and ceiling, provides more storage space than a freestanding one. Although an empty wall provides the most suitable site for a fitted wardrobe it is not essential. End panels allow you to circumvent windows and radiators and open shelves can span the space between.

Chimney breasts can be hidden within the cupboard if internal fittings are planned to follow the changing depth. A ready-made sliding door kit makes installing the cupboard simple and allows you to decide on the internal depth you want. Remember to allow clearance between internal fittings and the back of the door panels of at least 100mm (4in) (see page 52 for installation instructions).

You can organize the interior space to suit your particular mix of clothing with shelves, drawers or baskets, hanging rails and shoe racks. A section that takes two rails one above the other for short length clothing like jackets and shirts uses space economically. List the items you want to store then choose fittings to suit. Fitting out the interior is dealt with on page 54.

If you want your fitted cupboard to blend with the rest of the room, paint or paper the doors to match the room scheme. Mirrored doors will add light and a feeling of space.

Rather than using the complete wall you may prefer to incorporate a dressing table, vanitory unit or chest of drawers – see opposite page for some suggested arrangements.

Where space around the bed is limited fix a small shelf on brackets on either side of the bed to take bedside lighting, a clock, book and other bedside paraphernalia.

Alternative fitted wardrobe arrangements

A Use end panels to give two equal-sized cupboards with a centrally situated vanitory unit for make up, shaving and wash space.

B Central space left between two cupboards can also provide a bed-sized alcove. Span the space at ceiling height with shallow cupboards that can be used for items in irregular use, such as luggage.

C A unit could run along three-quarters of the wall and full-width shelves cover the rest to provide space for a small television and stereo equipment plus books and photographs.

D A wall with a window can be given fitted cupboards on either side. A deep shelf under the window, with storage space below hidden behind doors, is used as a window seat.

Using alcoves

Alcoves add character to a room and are easy to use for open shelving. If you want to provide a working area in your bedroom then an alcove is an ideal spot. Make a desk to fit the space, using a two-drawer filing cabinet and a worktop. Fix the worktop to a batten screwed to the wall at one end and the filing cabinet top at the other. Add shelves above.

It is also comparatively simple to use alcove space for a floor-to-ceiling cupboard that will take hanging storage along its length (see instructions on page 39). Both alcoves can be used in this way. One cupboard could contain full-length hanging space with a shelf above, the other could hide an old chest of drawers. A second rail fixed above this would provide hanging space for shorter items. The chimney breast, now transformed into a shallow alcove, could be used for further storage or for the bed.

Using fireplace space

It is a major job to remove a chimney but extra space can be released if the fireplace and surround is removed. By extending the height of the opening (with professional advice) it will take tall furniture. Use it for a chest with mirror above to act as a dressing table, or a bedroom chair (see page 65 for removing a fireplace).

Corner fittings

Corner shelves or a cupboard can often be fitted in where there is room for little else (see pages 45–47 for construction).

Left: *Mirrored wardrobe doors make a small bedroom seem twice its actual size.*

Above: A deep cupboard can hide a shower, taking the strain off a busy bathroom.

Right: The space between cupboards on a window wall can be used to create a seating area.

Smartly designed corner shower cubicles are now available that will not look out of place in a bedroom. As well as taking the pressure off the bathroom in the early morning rush hour, a shower also contributes to an invigorating start to the day. If you intend to install it yourself, see *Plumbing and Central Heating*, also in this series.

The space under the bed

Do not forget this hidden space – it may not be very high but a double bed takes up 3 sq m (3½ sq yd) of floor area and that is a third of the average-sized bedroom!

Shallow rectangular plastic boxes on castors are available to make underbed storage easy. A cheap alternative is to use wooden fruit crates begged from the local greengrocer. Sand them down then paint them and finally screw castors to each corner.

Another alternative is to screw a frame to the underside of the wooden bed base as a support for drawer or basket runners.

Space-saving furniture

The bed takes up the largest part of the floor area in most bedrooms and so choosing one that contracts to become a sofa or pivots up into a vertical position during the day will free space for an alternative use.

A spare bedroom, used only rarely for guests, could double up as a study, music room, playroom or quiet reading room. If you choose a sofa bed for regular daily use it is wise to spend the extra money on buying one with a sprung base to give good support. There is no bed-making involved if you pick one that folds up with sheet and under-blanket in place (duvet and pillows can be stored in a chest).

A bed that pivots up against the wall can also be put away ready made up as straps hold the bedding in place. Incorporate this in your fitted wardrobe if you want to hide it from view during the day.

Redundant baby's room

If your home includes amongst its small bedrooms one tiny room, too small for a bed, which the baby has grown out of, consider its use as a large, walk-in family closet. Fix rails along one wall, and a basket storage system along another. You could also use secondhand shop rails.

A small room next to the main bedroom could be turned into an en suite bathroom if a doorway is made between the two.

TIPS
- Sliding doors use up a minimum of floor area but only allow you to see part of the interior at a time.
- Folding panels or louvres on runners use up more width inside the cupboard (allow for this in construction), but provide a wider view.
- Hinged narrow panel doors use no interior space but open out to cover more floor area. These also provide a good view of the interior.
- Roller or louvre blinds can be raised for an overall view but these do not provide the same dust-resistant barrier.

CHILDREN'S ROOMS

A child's room needs to be colourful and fun and to mirror the owner's interests. It also needs surfaces that are tough and practical. In most cases the number of belongings expands at a surprising rate, requiring an adaptable storage system that is easy to use so there is some hope that things will be put away when they are no longer needed. Beds stacked on furniture, or raised on scaffolding reached by a ladder, are popular with many children and this arrangement leaves more floor space free for play. Furniture also needs to be adaptable so you can rearrange it as the child develops and interests change. A few additions can change the room into a teenager's bedsitting room.

Storage units

A tough, well secured, adjustable shelving system is probably the most practical way to store children's belongings. Wide lower shelves can be used to house brightly coloured plastic boxes which could be colour-coded according to their contents. Simple silhouette shapes painted on the wall behind are an alternative method of reminding the owner of what belongs where.

Industrial metal shelving is a practical alternative to shelves fixed to the wall. Your local car body repair shop should be able to spray this almost any colour you want.

Instead of pictures, hang animal shape pocketed storage and large fabric bags on the wall to hold small objects and soft toys.

Worktops

A good-sized working surface is useful for children of all ages. It provides space to bath and change a baby, room for a young child to crayon, paint and do jigsaws and for a schoolchild to study, do homework, make models or follow a number of other interests.

A chest of drawers and floor cupboard of equal height could form the base (here is a use for redundant kitchen units, brightly painted). Add a length of melamine-covered chipboard or kitchen worktop the width of the units. This is fixed to the units at each end, leaving a knee-hole in the middle. Extra units could extend the fitting along the full length of one wall.

Sleeping arrangements

Bunk beds These are a good sleeping arrangement even for a single child, as they provide space for a

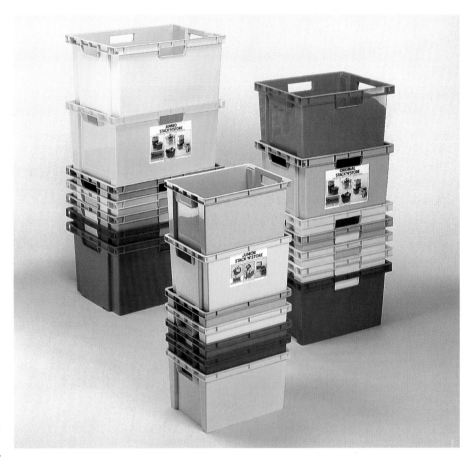

Above: Bright plastic boxes can be colour planned according to type of contents.

friend to stay and for extra daytime seating (see page 69).

Stacking beds One of the beds has folding legs and slides away unseen beneath the other. They are another useful alternative for an occasional guest.

Platform beds These provide space for storage below and can be placed against a wall or used as an island. The supports for the bed take up a minimum of floor space and so the system is ideal for small rooms.

A simple method of making a platform bed is to use those redundant kitchen units again, and a timber frame bed with the legs removed. You will need to secure a 100mm (4in) batten the length of the bed firmly to the wall at bed height. Then line the units up in front of this and far enough away from the wall to form the front edge. You can add a short ladder at the back for climbing into bed. If the units are not the right width you can fix a rail to fill the space which you can use for clothes hanging. Then fix the bed base firmly to the batten at the back and the unit work surface at the front. For a small child add a sur-

rounding rail to the bed but make sure that the height of the rail does not allow a child to slide, then get stuck, underneath it.

You could adapt the instructions for the bunk bed (see page 69) to make a platform bed with cupboards beneath.

Space below a bed can also be used for shallow storage boxes on castors.

Extras

To avoid walls being covered with original artworks it is a good idea to supply drawing space. You can make a large pad from scrap paper attached with giant clips to a thin rod or garden cane then hung from the wall. Paint a section of wall with blackboard paint to form a special scribbling spot.

If wall space is at a premium

Above: Scaffolding can be used to build an exciting work area plus bed platform.

Right: Large floor cushions, tied together, can be used for daytime seating or an extra bed.

make a simple easel-style drawing board. Use two equal-sized sheets of 12mm (½in) thick medium density fibreboard. Attach battens to the back down each side, extending them at one end to form legs. Attach hinges to join the top sides and use two lengths of heavy duty tape to hold the board in its extended position. One side could be painted with blackboard paint, the other used for drawing paper.

A hard floor is the most practical surface for many games. Boards can be covered with ply or chipboard sheets to provide some insulation and these can be painted with a series of designs for use with specific games. Alternatively, street and countryside scenes would provide a background for the use of vehicles and farmyard animals.

Teenagers' rooms

Older children feel a need for independence and many want to entertain their friends in their own sitting room. A bed length bolster and cushions can turn a bed into a daytime sofa. Large floor cushions can provide extra seating for friends, then be stacked in a corner when out of use. You could make a low coffee table from a square of blockboard with empty paint tins screwed on in each corner for legs.

Bear in mind sound insulation when items are being positioned. This can, to some extent, be provided by shelf-stored items, a cork noticeboard and a fitted carpet. The position of speakers is also important.

SAFETY POINTS
Small children are best supplied with lighting that is out of reach but with easily accessible switches. A dimmer switch allows lighting to be lowered and still provide some night-time glow. Use special push-in covers on sockets throughout the house. Child-safe paint with a low lead content should be used for renovating furniture and toys.

BATHROOMS

Nearly always the smallest room in the house and the one that everyone wants to use at the same time, the bathroom needs clever planning. A shower or extra basin in the largest bedroom, or under the stairs, could relieve the pressure of the morning rush hour. A vanitory or shelving unit can provide storage for larger items, while hanging shelves and baskets can take the smaller ones.

Planning the space

Even if you intend to replace the bathroom fittings when you move into a new home it is a good idea to start by living with the present ones. This is the only way you can judge whether they are in a convenient position.

When buying new fittings remember that bright or deep coloured sanitaryware will make a small room appear more cluttered. Deep colours need constant cleaning too!

Improving the bathroom bottleneck

It is reckoned that it takes on average 15 minutes to have a bath and 4 minutes to have a shower, so installing a shower saves on time as well as fuel.

Right: *Where there is space, two basins can alleviate the morning rush period.*

Below: *In a tiny bathroom there may only be space for storage in a tall unit.*

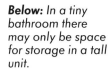

The easiest way to provide a shower is to replace standard bathtaps with a bath/shower mixer. If you would prefer a separate cubicle but space is tight consider replacing the present bath with a short sit-up design, so releasing more floor space for a shower cabinet.

Could a shower be fitted into the cloakroom, the corner of a bedroom or a landing corner? If a suitable spot is close to the 'wet end' of the house (bathroom and kitchen) the plumbing will be easier and less expensive.

An extra basin could be another time saver. Could you replace the present pedestal basin with a wall-to-wall unit in which two basins would slot?

What about the bedrooms? Installing a vanitory unit in the bedroom of a bathroom hog could considerably relieve the problem.

Finding storage space

Replacing a pedestal basin with a vanitory unit is one way of providing storage space (see page 67 for instructions). Apart from buying a kit or building your own cupboard to take the basin you can also use an old or decorative piece of furniture – for example, a Victorian sideboard. The top could be replaced with a marble-look kitchen worktop and a basin fitted into one end. A mirror placed on the wall above the other end would make that section into a good-sized make up and shaving spot.

You could provide additional storage space by using a freestanding storage unit to section off the lavatory from the rest of the bathroom (instructions for building a unit are on page 42). Hanging shelves placed out of the way high on the wall could hold spare soaps, shampoo and other small containers. Use translucent perspex for the shelves and clear plastic for the slings to create a see-through system.

QUICK TIP
Install a series of hanging baskets on hooks screwed into the ceiling joists along part of the side of the bath. Place one at a height that is easily accessible from the bath. Plants could provide a partial screen and the lowest basket could be used for sponge, nail brush, shampoo, bath oil and so on.

OUTDOORS

A well-fitted-out garage or garden shed can provide useful additional storage that will lighten the load on space in the house. Make sure these areas are well secured, particularly if used for tools. A small lean-to conservatory could act as a utility room, taking overspill from a small kitchen.

Garage storage

Most garages, unless they fit your car like a glove, allow space for overspill storage from the house. A system of special roof hooks can take stored timber and boards horizontally at roof level. Giant wall hooks allow you to hang ladders, bicycles, and other large items out of the way off the ground. A series of shelves can take bottled jams, wines and wine-making equipment, as well as car accessories and DIY tools.

Use any available floor space for a large freezer or a work bench. If the garage is attached to the house and space is tight in the kitchen consider installing a washing machine and tumble dryer in the garage too.

Using a garden shed

A shed provides useful additional storage space and, if it has good-sized windows, can be used as a workshop. If you want a shed you can work in remember to choose one with the door positioned to one side, allowing more space for a workbench. A centrally positioned door is best when the shed is to be used for storage only as this provides space for a waist level shelving unit at one side and hooks to take mower, garden chairs and long-handled tools at the other. If space is very tight a 1m (3ft) square shed with double doors will provide shallow, easy to get at storage space.

Finding space in a conservatory

By glazing over a passageway down the side of a house, or building a small lean-to conservatory around the back door, space protected from the weather becomes available to house laundry equipment or a freezer. Shelves on the house wall could take flower vases and jugs. You could also add a coat and wellie rack (see page 93 for details of hooks).

Left: Hooks, clips and adjustable shelves can turn a garage into a useful and efficient storage area.

PART 2

DOING THE WORK

Turn plans into reality with plenty of easy-to-follow instructions for specific storage and space-saving projects such as:

■ How to put up shelves in a variety of situations with a selection of fixing methods.

■ How to put together a freestanding shelf or corner unit.

■ How to make a fold-down table, vanitory unit or bunk bed.

■ How to fit wall-to-wall or alcove cupboards.

■ How to rehang a door to allow for better use of the surrounding area.

■ How to fit a loft ladder and loft flooring to make better use of loft space.

SHELVING SYSTEMS

Shelves can be made to serve a variety of purposes, from storing tools and pots of paint in the garden shed to displaying books and houseplants in the living room. The vast range of supports and materials available means that you should not have trouble in finding something that matches your needs. If colour is important to suit the decor of a room, you can always paint or stain a shelving system to suit, otherwise choose a steel or plastic coated system that is already coloured.

Types of support

The simplest type of shelf support is the angle bracket. The least expensive designs are L-shaped and are designed to be purely functional. Scrolled brackets are more attractive but this is reflected in their price. Brackets come in a range of sizes and can support virtually any type of shelving material (see below and right).

Adjustable steel and aluminium shelving systems are made by several manufacturers and are an excellent choice if you think you may want to alter the height or depth of the shelves in the future. With these systems, special brackets are clipped into slotted uprights that are screwed to the wall. The uprights are available in a selection of lengths and the brackets come in sizes from 100mm (4in) to 300mm (12in).

Wooden adjustable shelves are a popular alternative to their steel counterparts because they are considerably more appealing to the eye. The least expensive types comprise brackets that are pegged into softwood uprights.

If you want to tailor-make a shelving system, perhaps to fit into an alcove, you can make supports out of 50mm × 25mm (2in × 1in) battens.

Types of shelving material

Melamine-faced chipboard (Contiboard) is one of the most popular shelving materials because it is comparatively cheap and is easy to wipe clean. You can buy Contiboard in large sheets that you can then cut to size yourself or you can buy it in a selection of widths as ready-made shelves. Thicknesses vary, but for most purposes 15mm (⅝in) boards are sufficient provided they are adequately supported. If you do cut boards to size buy iron-on strips to

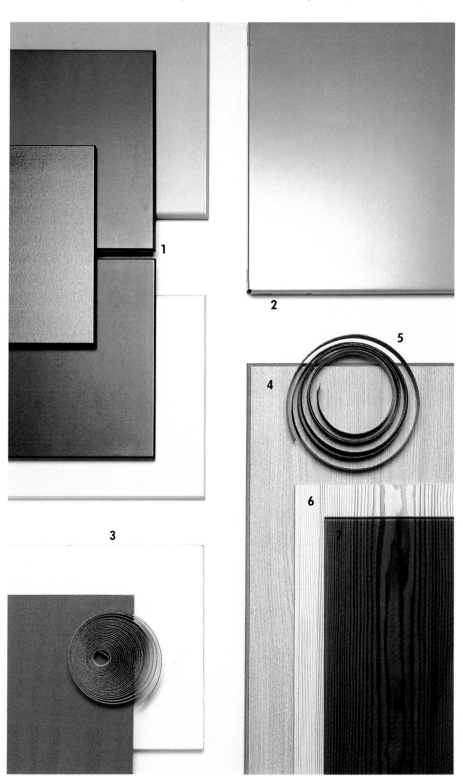

cover the sawn edges.

Similar to melamine-faced Contiboard is veneered chipboard which looks like solid timber but costs far less. Veneered boards should always be sealed with a varnish or else the veneer may lift off if it gets damp.

Planks of wood are a good choice for shelving, particularly where strength is required. Common thicknesses range from 12mm to 25mm (½in to 1in) and planks come in a choice of lengths and widths. When buying planks, make sure that they are straight and do not have any loose knots in them. Where appearance is not important, chipboard, blockboard and plywood are practical alternatives to solid wood.

Specially toughened glass can be used to make shelves provided the corners have been rounded off and the edges ground smooth – jobs that are best left to an expert glazier. Steel shelves are usually sold as part of a kit that also includes the supports. Although they are not particularly attractive, steel shelves are tough and are therefore a good choice if heavy or bulky items are to be stored off the ground.

Another material which is increasingly popular for shelving is MDF (medium density fibreboard). It is available faced with melamine, or unfinished if you prefer to paint it to match other woodwork.

Types of edging

Finishing off wooden shelves with edging can serve two purposes – it can strengthen the shelves and it can make them more appealing to look at. If extra support is required to prevent the shelves from bowing, battens or strips of steel or aluminium can be screwed either along the edges or on the underside. If appearances are more important, strips of moulding can be glued and pinned to the leading edges.

Shelving (left):
1. Pre-finished MDF, 2. Painted steel shelving, 3. Melamine-faced chipboard with edging strip, 4. Pre-finished wood-effect shelf, 5. Veneer edging strip, 6. Pine effect chipboard, 7. Tinted glass with polished edge

Brackets (right):
1. L-shaped angle bracket. 2. Adjustable wooden bracket and upright, 3. Adjustable steel system, 4. Wooden batten for alcove shelving, 5. Hanging shelf bracket

Edgings (far right):
1. Timber edging on veneered shelving, 2. D-shaped moulding on pineboard shelf, 3. Aluminium trim on melamine-faced chipboard, 4. Wooden batten to give extra support to melamine-faced shelf

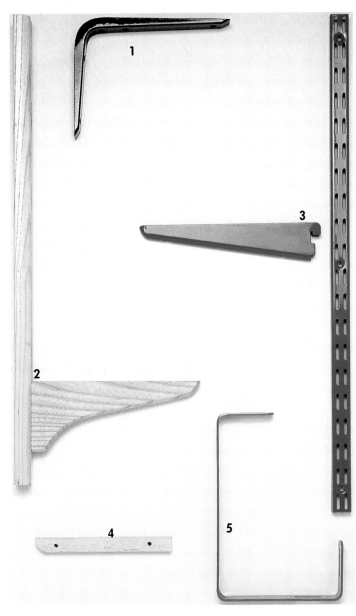

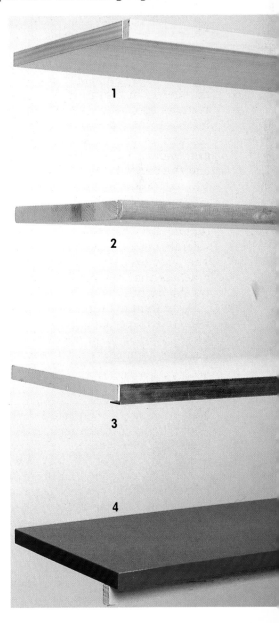

Bracket shelving

Tools and materials: screwdriver, pencil, bradawl, drill and masonry bits (for solid wall), spirit level, long rule (straightedge) or batten, 32mm (1¼in) No.8 woodscrews, 12mm (½in) woodscrews (for timber shelving) or chipboard screws (for Contiboard and chipboard), wallplugs (for solid walls), pair of brackets, shelving material.

Putting up shelving of any kind is made much easier, especially when it comes to checking that the levels are right, if two people do the job – so arrange for some help if possible.

Start off by marking the ideal positions of the two brackets on the wall (1). Check that the brackets are level with each other by laying a spirit level on top of a straightedge that spans the gap between the two. When postioning the brackets, bear in mind that if the span between them is too great, the shelf may sag. As a rough guide, 25mm (1in) thick softwood should be supported every 900mm (3ft) or so, whereas chipboard of similar thickness needs to be supported about every 750mm (2½ft). If you are planning to put heavy items on the shelves, consider adding extra supports to take the weight. If possible, avoid fixing the brackets at the very ends of the shelf; it is better to bring them further in.

If you are fixing into a solid wall, drill holes for the screws using a masonry bit, insert wallplugs and then screw the brackets in place (2). If you are fixing into a partition wall, it is best to screw directly into the wooden studs inside the wall; this will probably mean changing the positions of the brackets slightly. Locate the vertical studs by tapping the wall with the handle of your screwdriver – a solid noise indicates a stud. See pages 80–84 for information on drilling and fixing.

If necessary, saw the shelving material to size and fit it to the brackets from underneath using either woodscrews or chipboard screws (3).

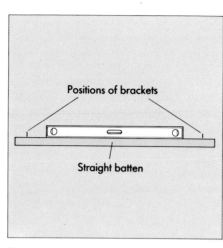

1 Mark the positions of the brackets on the wall, using a straight batten to make sure the marks are level.

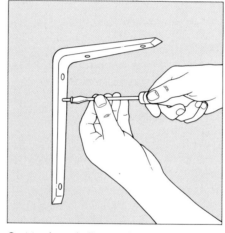

2 Mark drilling holes through brackets, then screw in place, plugging the wall first if necessary.

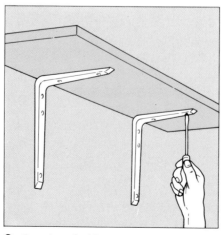

3 Cut the shelf to size, position on brackets, then secure it with screws driven up from beneath.

Alcove shelving

Tools and materials: screwdriver, tenon saw, jigsaw, glasspaper, tape measure, spirit level, try square, countersink, G-cramp, pencil, wood filler, 38mm (1½in) No.8 woodscrews, wallplugs, PVA wood glue, 25mm (1in) No.8 woodscrews, 50mm × 25mm (2in × 1in) battens, shelving material (timber).

Although it is possible to fix an alcove shelf with short battens at each end, it is usually better to add a batten along the back of the shelf as well to give extra support.

Pencil in the rough position of the shelf on the walls of the alcove. If you plan on adding a number of shelves, space them out carefully.

Once you have marked the position of a shelf, measure the width of the alcove at that level. The simplest way of doing this is to use the 'sliding batten' method: hold two straight battens together and slide them out so that the ends touch the side walls of the alcove (1). Clamp the battens together and then use them to mark the length of the shelf (2). It is always a good idea to take several measurements inside an alcove because the walls may not be perfectly parallel with each other.

Having marked out the shelf, cut it to length using a jigsaw. Smooth off the rough edges of the sawn timber with a sheet of glasspaper wrapped around an offcut of batten.

Next, measure and cut the back batten to length. Try it for size against the wall, checking that it is perfectly horizontal with a spirit level laid on top. When you are happy with the level of the batten, mark its position with a pencil (3).

The two end battens will match the width of the shelf less the thickness of the back batten. Mark them to length and then cut them to size with a tenon saw. It is a good idea to cut the front edges of the end battens at an angle of 45°. Mark the positions of the battens on the side walls of the alcove, checking that they are perfectly level.

The back battens should be fixed

with screws spaced at centres of 300mm (12in) or so. Drill clearance holes for the screws through the middle of the battens and then countersink them so that the screw heads will lie beneath the surface of the wood (4). The end battens should be fixed with at least two screws.

Hold each batten in place and mark the screw positions through the clearance holes. Drill holes in the walls for wallplugs, using a masonry bit (you will find it easier to drill the holes if you have a hammer facility on your electric drill). Fix the battens to the walls using 38mm (1½in) woodscrews driven into wallplugs (5).

The shelf itself is fixed to the battens with screws spaced out every 450mm (18in) or so. Drill out countersunk clearance holes for these screws, making sure that they are not more than 12mm (½in) out from the edge of the timber. Position the shelf on top of its supports and mark the battens through the clearance holes. Make pilot holes in the battens with a bradawl or a small drill. Lay a bead of PVA wood glue along the top of the battens and then fix the shelf in place with 25mm (1in) woodscrews. Cover up all the screw heads with a wood filler that is tinted to match the timber (6). When the filler has dried, rub it smooth with fine glasspaper.

Finally, it is a good idea to coat the shelf with one or two layers of varnish or paint. This will protect the wood from superficial damage and will also prevent it from getting damp and warping.

To give alcove shelving a built-in look, and to provide extra support and prevent the front edge from sagging, trim the front of the shelf with a length of timber 75 × 12.5mm (3 × ½in) fixed in place with 25mm (1in) countersunk woodscrews.

Another alternative is to edge the front of the shelf with architrave. Indeed, you can also use architrave to make the supporting battens themselves, as long as the shelves do not have to take a substantial amount of weight.

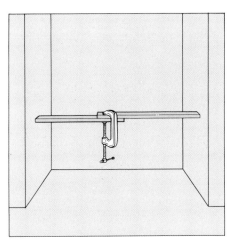

1 Slide the battens apart until they fit horizontally across the alcove, then clamp them together.

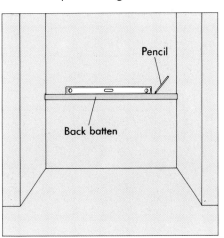

3 Mark the fixing position of the back batten, using a spirit level to check that it is horizontal.

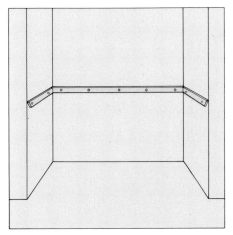

5 Drill and plug holes in the wall to take back batten. Screw in place. Repeat for the side battens.

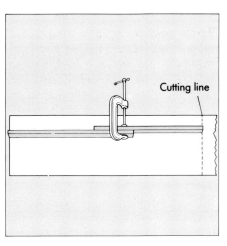

2 Use the clamped battens to transfer the width of the alcove to the shelf, and mark the cutting line.

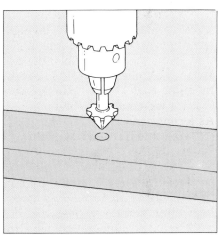

4 Drill countersunk holes through the back batten. Hold up batten and mark the wall through the holes.

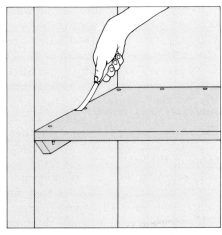

6 Fit the shelf, and screw in place from above. Cover the heads of the screws with wood filler.

Adjustable shelving

Tools and materials: screwdriver, spirit level, stud detector (partition wall), 32mm (1¼in) No.8 screws, (or as recommended), wallplugs (solid walls), measuring and marking tools, shelving and support kit.

It is important that the vertical supports are fixed securely because they take the brunt of the weight and stress put on the shelves. The spacing of the uprights depends on the material used for the shelves (see page 38). The outer brackets should be no more than 450mm (18in) from the ends of the shelves. For long shelves add extra supports. Measure a shelf and then mark the positions of the supports on the wall (1). If you are fixing into a partition wall, the supports should be fixed into the nearest studs; you can locate the studs with an electronic stud detector.

Fix the first support loosely to the wall by its top screw only (2). Let it hang and check that it is vertical with a spirit level (3). When you are satisfied, mark all the fixing holes and anchor the bottom of the upright with a screw. Before adding the rest of the screws, check that the upright is vertical in the other plane and if necessary, pack out behind the upright with strips of cardboard (4).

Place a bracket at the top of the upright and also put one in the corresponding slots on the second upright. Hold the second upright in position against the wall and then get a helper to lay a shelf on top. Check that the shelf is horizontal before marking the exact position of the second upright (5).

Fix the second upright as you did the first, drilling and packing it out before screwing in place, and then add brackets and shelves as required. On some systems the shelves are fixed to the brackets with clips or sticky pads but with others they are held by screws driven through the brackets from underneath (6).

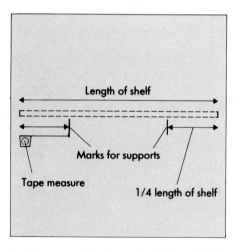

1 Measure the length of the shelf, and decide on bracket positions. Mark the spacing of the uprights.

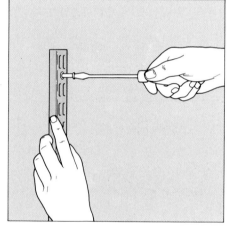

2 Mark the position of the top fixing point. Drill and plug the wall, then screw the upright in place loosely.

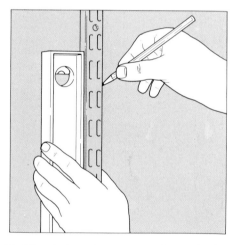

3 Check that the support is vertical, then mark, drill and plug the lower screw positions.

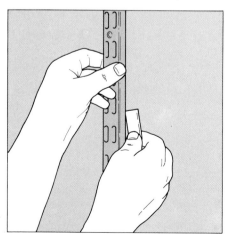

4 Check the upright is vertical in the other plane and pack it out with slips of cardboard if necessary.

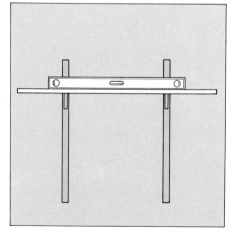

5 Fit brackets in each upright and add a shelf. When it is level, mark position of second support.

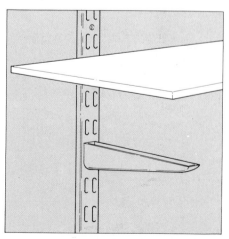

6 Fit second support as in steps 2–4, then add brackets and shelves, fixing with screws, clips or sticky pads.

Other types of shelving

Radiator shelves The easiest type to install has a Y-shaped support which rests on top of the radiator and uses the wall as a prop (1). The shelf lies on top of a pair or more supports and is held firm with sticky pads (2). Before installing this type of shelving, check that the radiator is securely fixed as anything put on the shelves will strain the fixings. Other types of radiator shelves are secured by clamps which make them more substantial but nevertheless the weight load is transferred to the radiator brackets. Shelves above radiators help to deflect heat into the room, and prevent unsightly marks caused by heat and dust.

Freestanding basket racks These are not strictly speaking shelving systems but they are extremely useful and can be used to store anything from clothes to books. The *Elfa* system uses self-assembly frames (3) which are easily assembled and come in a selection of sizes to suit most requirements. It is possible to clip frames together to create a comprehensive storage system. The baskets and shelves, which again come in a range of sizes, slide into runners that form part of the frame (4). Among the many accessories that can be added to a basket system are castors (which enable the entire system to be moved) and basket stops, which prevent the baskets from being pulled out of their grooves. Clothes rails can also be fitted to *Elfa* systems which means that they can be used as a wardrobe in a bedroom.

Steel shelving systems These allow for the shelves to be positioned at different heights within the framework (5). They are also sold as kits that contain everything you need apart from a screwdriver. Steel systems are not always very stable once they have been erected and tend to wobble if heavy items are placed on the top shelves so secure them to a solid wall with screws (6).

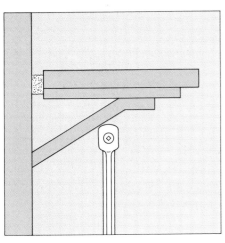

1 The simplest type of radiator shelf has Y-shaped supports which rest on top of the radiator.

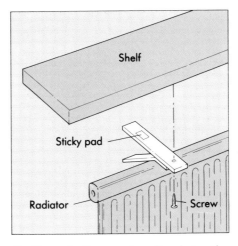

2 The shelf can be fixed to the brackets with screws. Fit draught excluder along the back of the shelf.

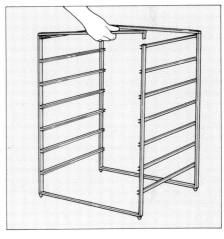

3 The Elfa storage system consists of self-assembly frames of runners and uprights which snap together.

4 A wide range of wire and plastic baskets and shelves slide into place on the framework.

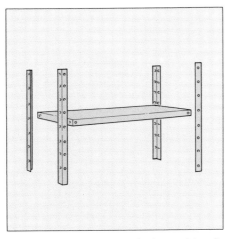

5 Shelves on steel shelving kits fit into angled uprights, allowing you to adjust the spacing.

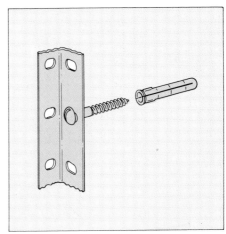

6 To make the shelving more stable, screw the uprights to the wall, packing out behind if necessary.

DIVIDER SHELF UNIT

This unit creates valuable storage space and at the same time it acts as a room divider. It is ideal if you want to separate off a dining room area in a large sitting room, for example, without cutting out all the light from the windows. You could even use it to divide up a child's bedroom. The basic design can be adapted to suit your requirements – you could for instance make made-to-measure compartments for a stereo system with space for records and tapes alongside.

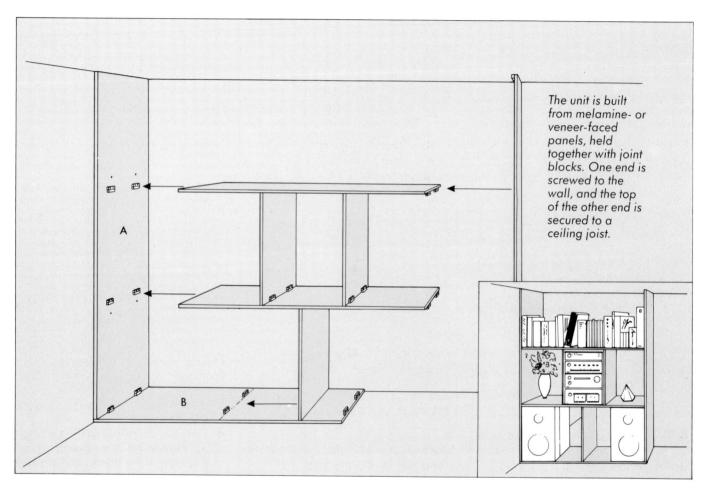

The unit is built from melamine- or veneer-faced panels, held together with joint blocks. One end is screwed to the wall, and the top of the other end is secured to a ceiling joist.

Tools and materials: jigsaw, screwdrivers, chalk line, bradawl, spirit level, try square, tape measure, joint blocks, 15mm (⅝in) faced chipboard, plastic screw covers, 38mm (1½in) woodscrews, wall-plugs, 19mm (¾in) chipboard screws.

The one thing to bear in mind when drawing up your modifications to the basic design is to provide adequate support for the shelves; chipboard is not very strong so place vertical dividers every 500mm (20in) or so. Another thing to watch out for is the width of the unit – a unit that is less than 300mm (12in) wide will probably not be of much practical value. Faced chipboard is available in sheets 300mm (12in) wide up to a length of 2440mm (8ft). To help you get the proportions right, it is a good idea to map out your design on squared paper using a scale of 1:20. Take into account the height of the ceiling and width and depth of the unit (1). At this stage, use a stud detector to locate the joist in the ceiling where the top of the unit will be anchored; you may have to modify your design slightly so that the end piece can be secured.

Mark out the area of the unit on the floor using a chalk line, remem-bering that one end of the unit should be attached to a solid wall (2). The unit can be erected over a carpet or other floor covering so there is no need to lift everything up if you are not re-decorating. Having marked out the floor area, check that it is square to the wall.

Mark the position of the end piece (A) on the wall and check that your lines are vertical with a spirit level. You may have to saw out a section of skirting board so that the unit can butt up tight against the wall.

The next step is to cut out all the shelves and dividers. Some of these will be the same size as each other so, having cut out one piece, you can

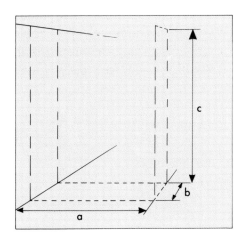

1 Measure up and plan the dimensions of the unit, taking into account the available sizes of the panels.

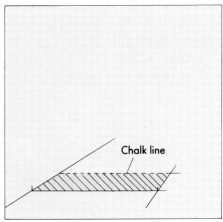

2 Use blackboard chalk to mark out the area of the unit on the floor: there is no need to lift floorcovering.

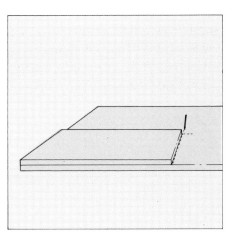

3 Cut out the sections. For sections the same size, use one as a template for marking the next.

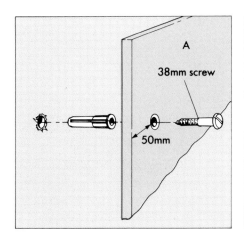

4 Fix the end panel to the wall, screwing directly into a stud wall or drilling and plugging a solid wall.

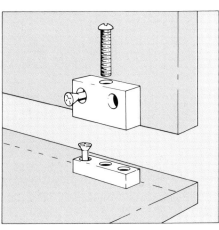

5 Fit base panel and join with joint blocks. Join uprights and shelves, using two blocks per joint.

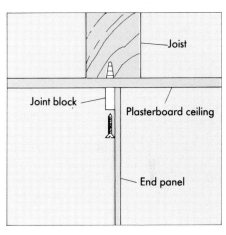

6 Fit the end upright to the ceiling. If using veneered chipboard, finish with two or more coats of varnish.

use it as a template to mark out others (3). It is quickest to use a jigsaw when it comes to cutting out the pieces.

One way to prevent the saw blade from shattering the veneer on the chipboard is to score the cutting line with a sharp handyman's knife. If you then cut to the waste side of the line, you will be left with a nice clean edge. See pages 74–75 for more information on using saws.

After you have cut out all the pieces, label them before going any further so that you do not get confused. Stand the end piece (A) on top of the base (B) and screw it to the wall through countersunk clearance

holes with 38mm (1½in) wood-screws and suitable wallplugs (4). You can either conceal these fittings with shelves later on or you can cover the screw heads with snap-on plastic plugs. With A and B in place, start to assemble the shelf and divider components. Joint blocks provide the easiest way of doing this although you could use dowels if you prefer. Two blocks per join should be sufficient provided they are fixed with chipboard screws. Mark the screw holes through the joint blocks with a bradawl, making sure that the blocks are about 50mm (2in) from the edges (5). When assembling the components, consider carefully

where you position the blocks – wherever possible, try to make sure that they are on the 'blind' side so that they will not be visible when the unit is completed.

You will probably need a helping hand when it comes to joining the shelves to the end supports. Have a friend hold the construction steady while you insert the fixings.

The final stage in the construction is to secure the end piece to the ceiling. Again joint blocks can be used for this. Fix the joint blocks to the upright with chipboard screws and to the joists with woodscrews. Varnish veneered chipboard to provide a tough finish (6).

SPEAKER AND TV BRACKETS

If your television set or stereo speakers currently occupy valuable shelf space, a canny way to make more room is to fit them to purpose-made wall brackets, thus creating more storage space for books and ornaments on the shelves. A television bracket consists of a hinged arm, with a supporting plate on the end, which can be swivelled back against the wall; speaker brackets have a slightly different design that allows the speakers to be tilted. Both types are fixed in much the same way.

Far left: A TV bracket lets the TV swing back against the wall when not in use.

Left: Speaker brackets allow the speakers to be angled towards each other.

Tools and materials: screwdriver, spirit level, drill and masonry bits, pencil, woodscrews, wallplugs, brackets.

It is best to screw these brackets, especially a television bracket which will have to take a considerable weight, to a solid wall so that you can get a really secure fixing. The best position for a television bracket is at about eye level when you are sitting in your favourite chair; speaker brackets on the other hand can be mounted higher up so that the sound can be 'focussed' towards the centre of the room or wherever you want. Before fixing either type of bracket, consider how you are going to conceal the wires that lead to the pieces of equipment. If they can be clipped behind shelves or run up a corner, so much the better.

When you have located the ideal position for a bracket, hold it against the wall and check that it is horizontal with a spirit level (1). Mark the wall through the screw holes with a pencil. Drill holes for the wallplugs with a masonry bit and screw the bracket in place. Use screws as recommended by the manufacturers, taking into account the weight of the equipment. Some manufacturers supply screws with the brackets.

Finally, secure the speaker or television to the bracket by way of the clamp that is usually tightened by a screw (2). Check that each bracket works smoothly and that it is securely anchored.

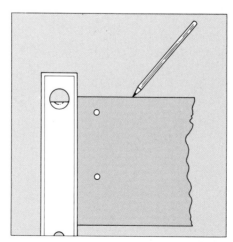

1 Mark the fixing positions of the bracket on the wall, checking that it is horizontal with a spirit level.

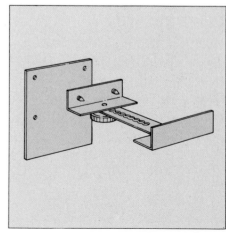

2 Tighten the knob underneath to clamp the cabinet firmly: nipping screws at the back add extra grip.

CORNER SHELVES

This set of shelves is designed to make the most of corner space which is often wasted or ignored altogether. The shelves can be fitted in a kitchen, living room or bedroom and a door can be added if you want to be able to hide things away. The design can be adapted to suit your needs. For example, you can add extra shelves or make the unit large or small, depending on what you want to store and the available space. If you want to add a door see pages 46 and 47.

Tools and materials: screwdriver, jigsaw or panel saw, combination square, steel straightedge, tape measure, drill and bits, countersink, plane or planer file, spirit level, glasspaper, PVA wood glue, 12mm (½in) plywood, two mirror plates, 12mm (½in), 25mm (1in) and 32mm (1¼in) No.8 woodscrews, wallplugs.

If you want to add a door, buy it first as it will determine the size of the unit (see pages 46 and 47).

Cut out the two back panels C and D from your sheet of plywood using a jigsaw. Fix the two panels together with PVA wood glue and countersunk 25mm (1in) screws spaced 150mm (6in) apart (1).

Mark out the A and B pieces and saw them to size (2). Screw and glue the shelves to the back panels.

Varnish or paint the unit before hanging it on the wall – this will add to its appearance and will protect it from damage.

Fix the two mirror plates along the top of the two side panels and then hang the unit using 32mm (1¼in) screws and wallplugs (3).

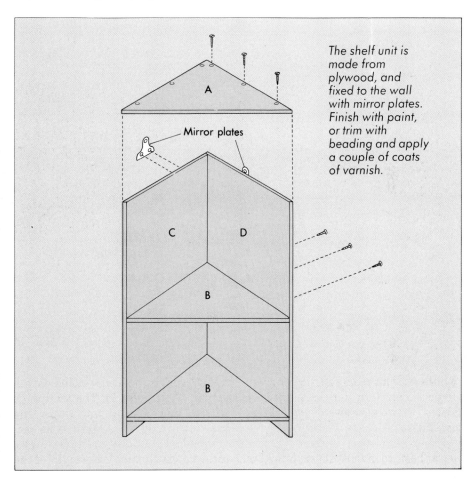

Mirror plates

The shelf unit is made from plywood, and fixed to the wall with mirror plates. Finish with paint, or trim with beading and apply a couple of coats of varnish.

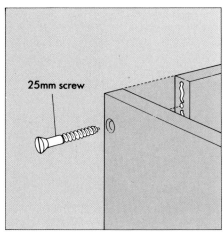

1 Cut out two back panels in plywood and fix them together at right angles, spacing screws 150mm apart.

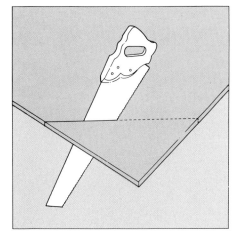

2 Cut out the shelf sections and the top panel, marking across the corners of the panel of plywood.

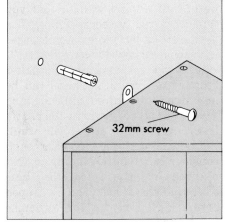

3 Fit the top panel and the shelves to the unit. Fix mirror plates at the top of the back panels; screw to wall.

ADDING DOORS TO CORNER SHELVES

If you add a door to the shelf unit on page 45, you create a corner cupboard which can look particularly stylish if you paint or varnish it. Ready-made louvre doors make life much simpler – there is a large selection of sizes and types available so you should be able to get exactly what you want. It is best to buy the door before you cut out and assemble the unit's components because the height and width of the unit will be determined by the size of the door.

Tools and material: in addition to the list on page 45, you will also need a marking gauge, a 12mm (½in) chisel, wooden mallet, handyman's knife, 38mm (1½in) brass hinges (with screws), 38mm (1½in) No. 8 woodscrews, magnetic catch (with screws), screw-in door knob (optional), louvre door, battening the same thickness as the door.

Once you have bought the door, you can assemble the unit as described on page 45, adjusting the size to take into account the width of the door and support battens.

When you have assembled the shelf unit, measure and cut the two battens that fit on either side of the door (1). The battens reach to the full height of the unit and are fixed to the shelves with 38mm (1½in) screws. Drill clearance holes in the battens for the screws and then mark through these into the shelves so that you can drill small pilot holes in the plywood.

The next step is to mark and cut the hinge recesses in the door and the support batten (2). Start marking the door first. The hinges should be spaced about 50mm (2in) of the way in from the top and bottom edges. To mark a hinge recess, you will probably find it easiest to use a marking gauge. With your marking gauge, measure the thickness and width of the hinge and transfer these readings to the edge of the door, bearing in mind that the knuckle of the hinge should lie in the middle of the edge of the door. The final stage is to chisel out the recess (3 and 4).

When you have cut out recesses in the door repeat the process on the door support batten.

Screw and glue the door supports to the shelf unit (6) and then hang the doors on the hinges (7) before fixing them to the support.

Position the magnetic catch under the bottom shelf where it will not be very noticeable. Make sure that the face of the catch is flush with the edge of the shelf before screwing it in place (8). Fix the catch plate to the door directly opposite the magnet.

It is not essential to fix a knob as you can use the bottom edge of the door to open and close. However, if you prefer to use a knob, start a hole first with a bradawl so that you don't split the wood (9).

A good finishing touch is to cover the countersunk screw heads with a filler so that all the surfaces are completely smooth. If you are going to paint the unit, use an ordinary cellulose wood filler but if you want to coat the unit with a transparent varnish or lacquer, it is best to use a tinted filler.

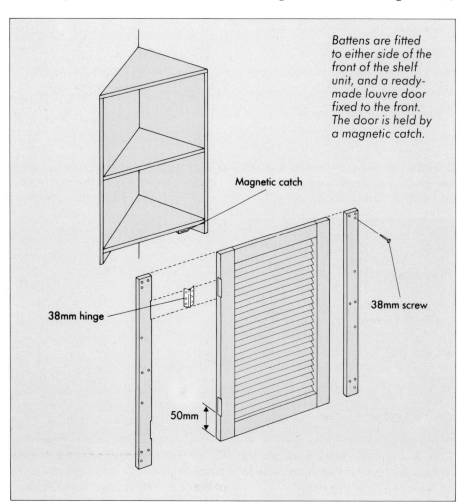

Battens are fitted to either side of the front of the shelf unit, and a ready-made louvre door fixed to the front. The door is held by a magnetic catch.

Magnetic catch

38mm hinge

50mm

38mm screw

USEFUL TIP

If you cannot find a tinted wood filler that exactly matches the colour of the timber, you can make up your own by mixing sawdust with PVA adhesive which is clear when it sets.

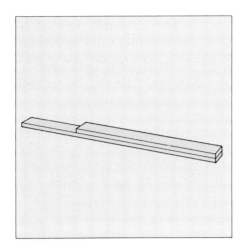

1 Cut a batten to match the height of the door, and use it to mark a cutting line for the opposite batten.

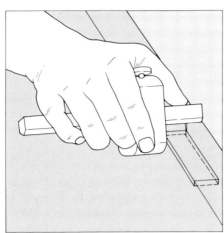

2 Use a marking gauge to scribe the outline of the hinges at the front of the edge of the door.

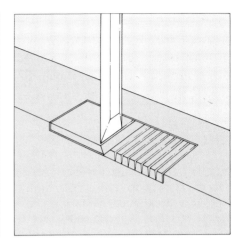

3 To chisel out the recess, first tap the chisel downwards to make a series of notches.

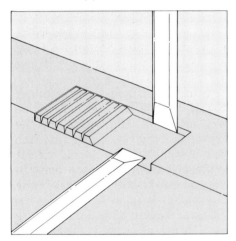

4 Tap down along the back edge of the hinge position, then chisel out the wood, working horizontally.

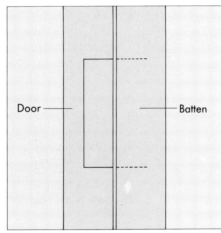

5 Hold the support batten against the door and mark hinge positions on edge of the batten. Chisel out.

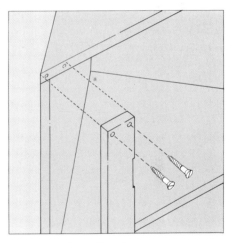

6 Screw and glue the door supports to the shelf and top of the unit, countersinking the heads of the screws.

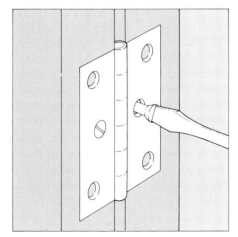

7 Screw the hinges to the door, then hold the door in place while you screw the hinges to the support.

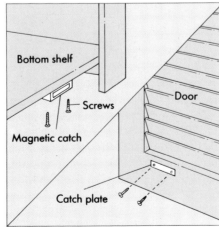

8 Fit a magnetic catch beneath the bottom shelf and a matching plate to the lower edge of the door.

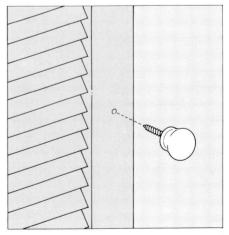

9 Screw a round wooden knob, or a metal or plastic D-handle to the front of the door, at a convenient height.

FOLD-DOWN KITCHEN TABLE

Kitchens are often cramped and short of space. A consequence of this is that there is often no room for a traditional kitchen table and no spare work surfaces when you are preparing large meals. This clever design gets over the problem – when you want to dine, you simply swing the table up; when you are short of space, you can fold it down out of the way. Although it looks complicated to make, do not be fooled – it is surprisingly easy to construct, using off-the-shelf items and a little ingenuity.

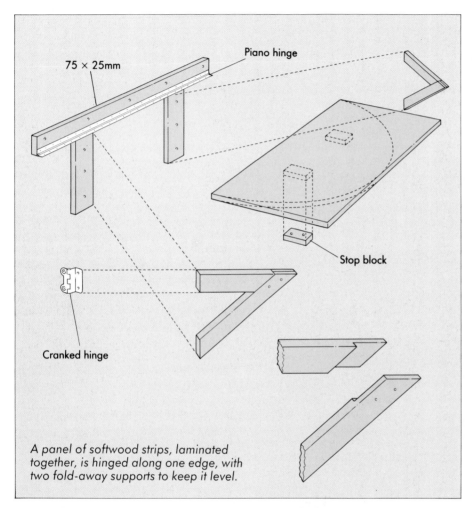

75 × 25mm

Piano hinge

Stop block

Cranked hinge

A panel of softwood strips, laminated together, is hinged along one edge, with two fold-away supports to keep it level.

Tools and materials: screwdrivers, tenon saw, panel saw, jigsaw, mitre box, tape measure, pencil, string, paint brush, hacksaw, spirit level, PVA wood glue, piano hinge, pineboard, varnish, 38mm (1½in) cranked hinges, 12mm (½in) No.4 woodscrews, 50mm (2in) and 25mm (1in) No.8 woodscrews, wallplugs, 75mm × 25mm (3in × 1in) softwood, 50mm × 25mm (2in × 1in) softwood.

The first task is to measure up the available space. If space is tight, a curved table is a good idea. Once you have decided on the size of the table, mark its position on the wall (1).

If you want a curved table, mark out the sweep with a piece of string anchored to a drawing pin and then cut out the shape from the sheet of pineboard with a jigsaw (2).

Next, measure and cut the base plate from a length of 75mm × 25mm (3in × 1in) timber – the base plate should be the same length as the table. The vertical supports are also cut from 75mm × 25mm (3in × 1in) timber and should be 600mm (2ft) long. Prepare these boards for fixing by drilling countersunk clearance holes through them at 150mm (6in) intervals.

The trickiest part of the whole job

is cutting and assembling the swing supports, especially the halving joints which should be angled at 45° – cut the angles in a mitre box with a tenon saw. The swing supports should reach out across at least half the width of the table and they should also be able to fold away neatly when not in use. Once you have cut the pieces to length, assemble the halving joints with PVA wood glue and 12mm (½in) wood screws (3).

Having cut out all the parts, it is a good idea to sand them prior to varnishing and painting – if you do not do this the table may warp due to steam in the kitchen (4). Pineboard is often sold pre-varnished but nevertheless, you should seal any sawn edges with at least two coats of clear varnish or lacquer. Leave each coat to dry for 24 hours before applying the next. Of course if you want to paint the timberwork, apply a primer first followed by two top coats (5).

Screw the wall base plate in place against your marks with 50mm (2in) screws driven into wallplugs (6). The vertical supports should be positioned about a quarter of the way in from the ends of the base plate. Hang the swing supports on 38mm (1½in) cranked hinges – these will allow the supports to fold tight against the wall (7). Make sure that the top hinges line up with the tops of the vertical supports.

Screw and glue the stop blocks to the underside of the table and then attach the piano hinge (8). If the hinge is too long, cut it to length with a hacksaw and smooth down any rough edges with a steel file. Finally, screw the hinge to the base plate using 12mm (½in) No.4 screws (9). The part of the hinge that is visible when the table is folded down can be disguised with paint.

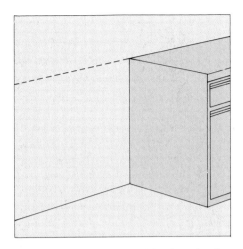

1 Decide on a suitable height for the table – to match the kitchen worktop – and mark a horizontal line.

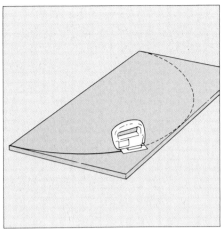

2 For a semi-circular table, mark out a cutting line on the pineboard and cut to shape using a jigsaw.

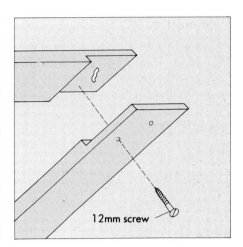

12mm screw

3 Cut and drill panels to hold supports, then make swing supports, using halving joints cut at an angle.

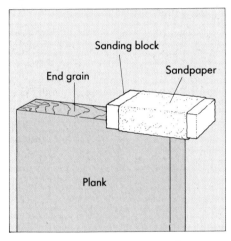

Sanding block

End grain   Sandpaper

Plank

4 Sand the table, especially sawn edges, to prepare the surface for varnishing or painting.

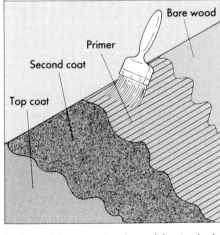

Bare wood

Primer

Second coat

Top coat

5 Varnish or paint the table, including cut edges, before final assembly, to seal the wood against moisture.

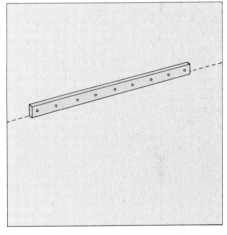

6 Screw pre-drilled and finished base plate to the wall, so that lower edge is level with marked line.

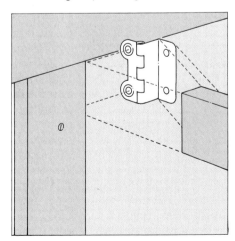

7 Fit uprights beneath base plate, about a quarter of the way in, then add supports on cranked hinges.

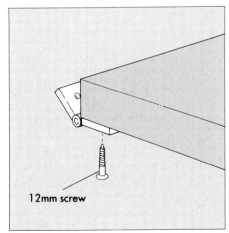

12mm screw

8 Fit stop blocks to the underside of the table, then fix the piano hinge along the back, underside edge.

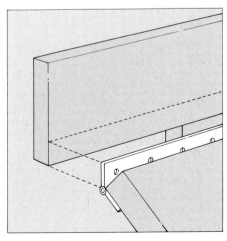

9 Screw the piano hinge in place along the front, lower edge of the wall batten, so table hinges down.

WALK-IN ALCOVE CUPBOARD

This original concept for a clothes cupboard makes the most of space to the side of a chimney breast. Inside the cupboard there is ample room for hanging clothes and storing shoes, or you could kit the interior out with alcove shelves (see pages 38 and 39) if you prefer. The design can be adapted to suit both your available space and your requirements but the first thing to do is choose a door as this will determine the size of the opening and could affect the design.

Tools and materials: tenon saw, panel saw, mitre box, claw hammer, tape measure, chalk line, chisels, plumbline, wooden mallet, spirit level, screwdrivers, combination square, handyman's knife, nail punch, PVA wood glue, 75mm × 75mm (3in × 3in) PAR softwood, 100mm × 25mm (4in × 1in) door lining, 25mm × 12mm (1in × ½in) door stop, skirting board, plasterboard, plasterboard nails, coving and coving adhesive (optional), door (complete with fittings), architrave, 75mm (3in) door hinges, 100mm (4in) wire nails, 25mm (1in) lost head nails, 25mm (1in) panel pins, 25mm (1in) No.8 woodscrews, 125mm (5in) No.12 woodscrews, wallplugs.

Mark out the area of the cupboard on the floor (you can build the cupboard over carpet) with a chalk line (1). If you are building up against a partition wall, bear in mind that the timber framework must be screwed into studs inside the wall – and to some extent this will determine the depth of the cupboard. At this stage it is a good idea to mark in the position of the door opening on the floor as well, taking into account the thickness of the door surround. Having marked out the floor, repeat the process on the ceiling – this is best done by dropping a plumbline down to your marks on the floor. Next, mark the wall for the position of the stud (on partition walls this must be fixed to a stud inside the wall).

Measure the vertical pieces of the framework to the height of the ceiling and then secure one of them to the wall against your mark, using 125mm (5in) screws spaced out at 300mm (12in) intervals (2). If you are fixing into a solid wall, do not forget to insert wall plugs.

Wedge the second framework stud in position, making sure that it is vertical in both planes – this will enable you to measure and cut all the other pieces accurately.

Having sawn all the other framework pieces out, skew-nail them together (3). For extra support, it is worthwhile screwing the pieces that run along the ceiling to joists. (4)

Cut sheets of plasterboard to size with a handyman's knife and nail them to the framework at 300mm (12in) intervals using special plasterboard nails (5). Fix the plasterboard with the cream side facing outwards so that it can be decorated over. The plasterboard around the door opening should be flush with the framework.

The door lining pieces are simply nailed to the framework with 25mm (1in) lost head nails spaced out at 300mm (12in) intervals. The lining should come flush to the edge of the

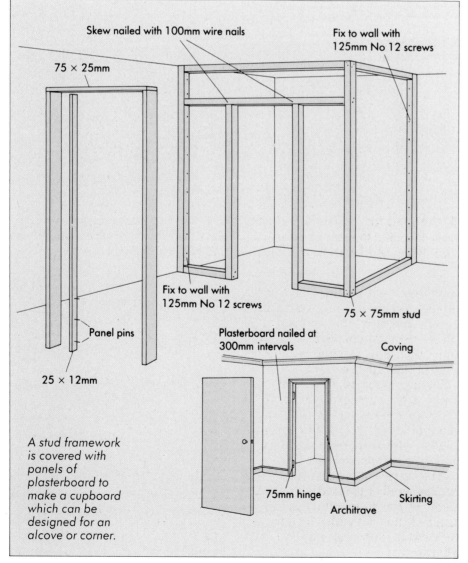

Skew nailed with 100mm wire nails

Fix to wall with 125mm No 12 screws

75 × 25mm

Fix to wall with 125mm No 12 screws

75 × 75mm stud

Panel pins

25 × 12mm

Plasterboard nailed at 300mm intervals

Coving

75mm hinge

Architrave

Skirting

A stud framework is covered with panels of plasterboard to make a cupboard which can be designed for an alcove or corner.

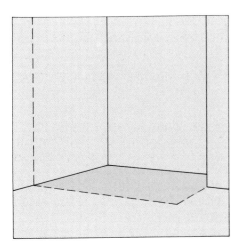

1 Decide on the overall size of the cupboard, taking note of any stud positions, and mark out the area.

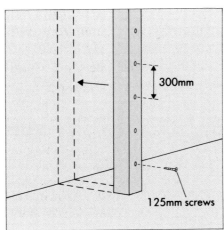

2 Cut vertical 75 × 75mm studs, and fix the first against the wall, using 125mm screws every 300mm.

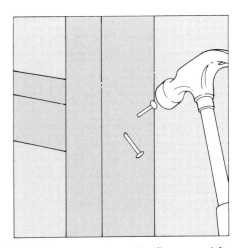

3 Fix battens along the floor, and fit remaining studs, including cross piece above door, by skew nailing.

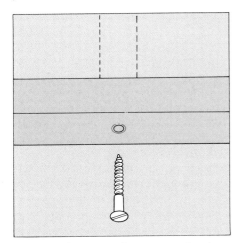

4 Fit timber to ceiling, screwing into a ceiling joist. Check for wiring before screwing into walls or ceiling.

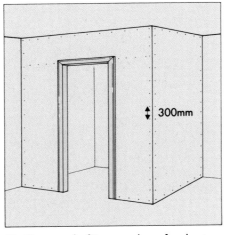

5 Cut and fit panels of plasterboard, so that they are flush with the door lining. Add architrave.

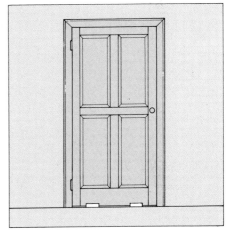

6 Fit hinges to door and wedge it in place to mark surround. Hang door and fit knob and catch.

plasterboard. Tap the nail heads beneath the surface of the wood with a nail punch and hammer.

Hold the door in the opening, flush with the edges of the lining, and, from the inside, mark the position of the door stop lengths. Remove the door and pin the door stops in place.

To fit the door, first wedge it in position, allowing for a clearance gap at the bottom, and mark the hinge positions, 150mm (6in) from the top and bottom. Then chisel out hinge recesses (see pages 46 and 47) and hang the door (6). The simplest type of catch to install is a spring-loaded nylon clasp.

Complete the door opening by sur-rounding it with architrave. Cut the angled corners in a mitre box with a tenon saw. Fix the architrave in place with 25mm (1in) lost head nails then nail skirting around the base of the cupboard.

Coving glued to the ceiling and walls of the cupboard rounds off the otherwise sharp angles. Most coving manufacturers sell special templates which enable you to make neat joins around corners (7).

The outside of the cupboard can be wallpapered or painted to match the decor of the room, while the inside can be kitted out with a hanging rail screwed to the two side walls or with shelves.

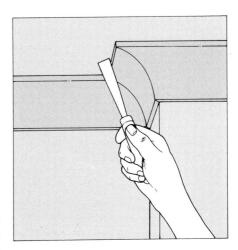

7 Finish by fitting coving and skirting, filling cracks before decorating to match the room.

SLIDING DOOR WARDROBE

If you have a bedroom that is cluttered up with chests of drawers and freestanding cupboards, you will be amazed at how much space you can gain in the room by replacing them with a sliding door wardrobe. For one thing, you will be able to use the area from the floor right up to the ceiling! Sliding door wardrobe kits are available in a variety of sizes that can reach up to 2.5m (8ft), or even more if you install a filler strip to make up the difference in height.

Below: *Wardrobe kits can be fitted into an alcove or add an end panel so they fit into a corner.*

Left: *Mirrored sliding door wardrobes provide excellent storage and at the same time create an illusion of space.*

Tools and materials: panel saw or jigsaw, hacksaw, plumbline, tape measure, screwdrivers, try square, steel straightedge, spirit level, chalk line, drill and bits, bradawl, wardrobe kit (including mirror door panels), 15mm (⅝in) melamine-faced chipboard panel (optional).

Two-, three- and four-door kits are available and they contain everything you need including runner tracks and screws. In addition to the basic kit, you will need mirror door panels. These come with a variety of trims, including gold, ivory, white, and brass so you should not have trouble in finding something that meets your fancy. Mirror finish doors reflect light and are therefore a good idea if you want to give the illusion of space within a room – they can actually give the impression that a room is twice the size it really is!

There are a variety of ways you can equip the inside of a wardrobe to make maximum use of the space (see page 54).

The first step is to measure the height of the ceiling and the area that you want the wardrobe to cover on the floor. It is simplest to install a kit from wall to wall but it is equally possible to add an end panel of melamine-faced chipboard if you want the wardrobe to extend only part-way across the floor (1). Once you have measured up the area, buy a kit to suit with either two, three or four doors.

If you are fitting a side panel, cut it to size so that it reaches from floor to ceiling. With the help of a friend, hold the panel in position, checking that it is vertical with a spirit level, and mark the ceiling (2). Follow this by chalking a line on the floor where the bottom track and doors will go (3). (You can build a wardrobe kit directly over a carpet). Having marked the floor for the bottom track, drop a plumbline down to it from the ceiling at regular intervals. At each point, mark the ceiling so that you know where the top of the wardrobe will be.

Using a hacksaw, cut the tracks to length (4), following the manufacturers' instructions.

Screw the top track to the ceiling joists with the screws provided (5). To find the joists, first tap the ceiling: a solid thud will indicate a joist. Confirm the location of a joist by poking a bradawl through the plasterboard, or lath and plaster – when you cannot push the bradawl in easily, you have confirmed the position of a joist. With the top track in place, screw the bottom track through the carpet, into the floorboards or subfloor (6).

Fit the hangers and runner guides to the door panels and attach the trims, which usually just snap on. Before hanging the door panels, kit out the inside of the wardrobe with dividers, shelves, rails and racks to suit your needs (see page 54). Hang the doors on the top rail and insert the runner guides into the bottom track. If needs be, adjust the doors until they run smoothly.

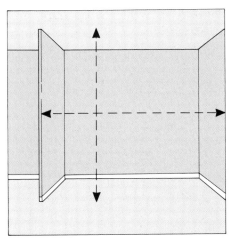

1 Measure up the area and decide on a position for the end panel if needed. Buy a kit to suit your needs.

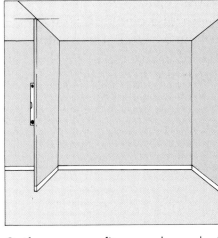

2 If necessary, fit an end panel of faced chipboard, checking that it is vertical with a spirit level.

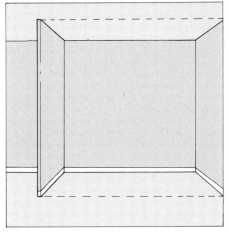

3 Mark the track position on the floor and ceiling, checking the marks are in line with a plumbline.

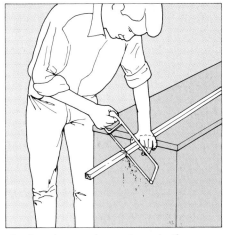

4 Cut the tracks to length if necessary, using a hacksaw. The tracks should fit inside the end panel.

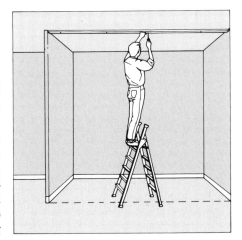

5 Tap the ceiling to find joists. Screw the top track to the ceiling, screwing into a joist.

6 Screw the bottom track in place to the subfloor. If this is concrete, use a hammer drill and plug the holes.

WARDROBE INTERIOR OPTIONS

Hanging rails

Many manufacturers produce hanging rail kits which are specifically designed to slot inside their wardrobe systems. The advantage of these kits is that they are easy to install and each pack contains everything you need. For large wardrobes, two or more kits can be joined together to fill out all the available space. Some kits have a double-rail format which allows you to double up on hanging space. If the ready-to-assemble kits do not suit your requirements, there is of course no reason why you should not erect your own system using conventional hanging rails and end fixings.

Shelves

Neat shelving systems are also made by wardrobe manufacturers and they can be used in conjunction with hanging rails. Shelving systems usually contain a number of drawers as well and with some types the shelves are adjustable. Provided there is enough space, alcove shelves (see pages 38/39) can be fitted inside a wardrobe. These are a good idea in tall wardrobes, where space is often wasted above the hanging rail. With a large wardrobe, it is perfectly feasible to build in a dressing table top. This could be fitted between two dividers that reach from the floor to the ceiling.

Storage baskets

A practical way of storing loose items is to put them into storage baskets. These come in a variety of colours and sizes – 545mm (21½in) baskets are probably the most convenient size as anything larger becomes too awkward to handle. The best way to support the baskets is on softwood battens screwed to divider panels. When installing a basket storage system, make sure that there is at least 50mm (2in) clearance between the top of one basket and the bottom of another otherwise they become difficult to pull out. (See also Basket racks on page 41.)

Plan the height of rails to suit the clothes you wear to ensure maximum use of space.

A shelving unit between two hanging areas provides useful storage for woollens or linen.

Wire baskets fitted to runners can be used beneath shelves, or between upright panels.

REHANGING A DOOR

Many doors are hung 'the wrong way round' or open in the 'wrong' direction, which can be both annoying and inconvenient. Rehanging a door is not as difficult as it sounds and it could gain you valuable space within a room and make access easier as well. Before you take a door off its hinges, consider exactly how you plan to rehang it as there are several options and some involve more work than others. You may need some matching paint to touch up superficial damage at the end of the job.

Tools and materials: pliers, screwdrivers, chisels, plane or planer file, wooden mallet, nail punch, pin hammer, try square, tenon saw, glasspaper, wood offcuts and wedges, wood glue, 25mm (1in) panel pins.

Changing sides

There are two ways you can change the side a door hangs – you can either turn the door around and adapt the locks and hinges, or you can swap the hinges and lock over and patch the holes that are left. Of the two methods, it is usually easier to turn the door around.

Remove the door by unscrewing the hinges from the door lining (1) – see overleaf. This is not always as easy as it sounds because layers of paint may make it hard to turn the screws. If this is the case, hold the screwdriver in a screw slot and tap the end with a hammer – the shock should loosen the screw and chip off the paint. Always remove the bottom hinges first and prop the door up on wedges so that it will not slip when the last screw is removed.

After lifting away the door, patch the hinge recesses in the door frame with offcuts of wood (2 and 3). If you make the patches slightly oversize you can trim them down until they are a tight fit. Pin and glue the patches in place, making sure that you tap the pin heads below the surface of the wood.

Release the door handles and pull out the spindle before undoing the screws that hold the lock or latch in place (4). Pull out the lock with a pair of pliers (5) and then test fit the door, the new way round, in the opening. Wedge the bottom of the door off the ground, at the same time making sure that it is clear at the top and at the sides. If necessary, trim the door with a plane until it fits properly.

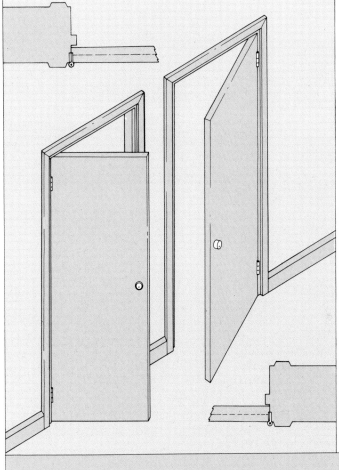

It is often possible to make better use of space in a room, or get better access, if the door is re-hung with the hinges on the opposite side. Either swap the sides of the hinges and catch, repairing redundant recesses, or rotate the door – you will still have to adjust the positions of the hinges and may have to turn the catch mechanism the other way up. Bear in mind that you may have to move the light switch so you can reach it as you enter the room.

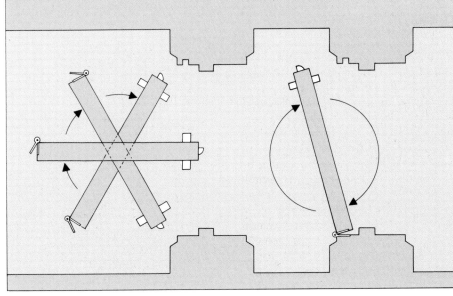

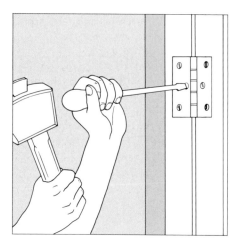

1 Remove the door by unscrewing the hinges from the surround. Use a mallet to clear layers of paint.

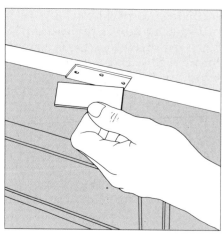

2 Remove the hinges and cut offcuts of wood a little larger than the hinge recesses.

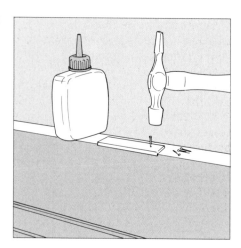

3 Fix the offcut with glue and pins, then trim away excess wood. Repeat for hinge recesses on the surround.

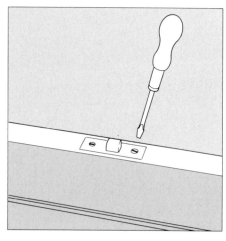

4 Remove handles and spindle, then remove the screws which hold the door catch mechanism in place.

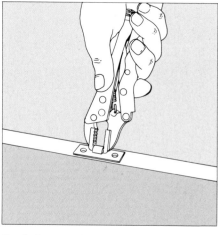

5 If the catch does not come out easily, use a pair of adjustable pliers to grip the latch and ease it out.

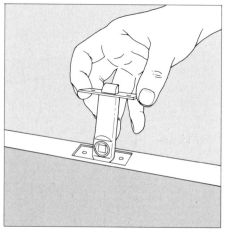

6 Check the door fits, then fit hinges and re-fit the lock, using the original lock and opening if possible.

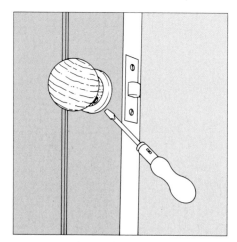

7 Re-fit the door handles (or use new ones if preferred). They are fixed by a grub screw.

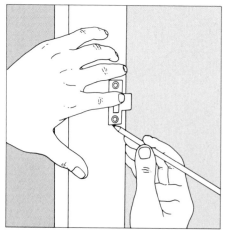

8 Close the door and turn the handle so the latch marks the jamb. Hold the plate in position. Mark all round.

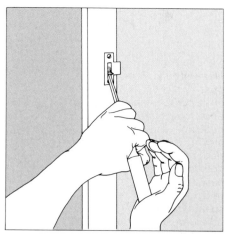

9 Chisel out a recess for the latch plate, with a deeper recess to accept the latch itself.

Before you refit the door, remove the lock striking plate from the frame. Patch the hole that is left with an offcut; it is best to avoid using filler as it will tend to slump and the results will not be as good. You must also adjust the hinge recesses on the door because they will be facing the wrong way. The simplest way of doing this is to chisel out the back of the recesses until you are left with a shallow slot, the depth of a hinge, right across the edge of the door. Always chisel towards the centre of the door or else the face of the door may splinter. Test fit a hinge in its new position and then patch up the redundant recess with an offcut.

Wedge the door in the opening the new way round and mark the new hinge positions on the frame. Remove the door again and chisel out the hinge recesses. Fit the hinges to the door and then hang the door in the frame, fixing the top hinge first.

Before refitting the lock or latch, confirm that it will work the other way round (6). With some types, you can just turn the striking latch – the curved piece that springs in and out – around but this is not always the case and you may have to buy a new lock. Once you have refitted the original lock or installed a new one, replace the door knobs (7). Turn the handle a few times so that the striking latch marks the door jamb.

Open the door again and hold the striking plate against the mark left by the latch. Mark around the plate (8). Chisel out the timber inside the marks to the depth of the plate and then fix the plate in place using the original screws. With the plate firmly attached to the door, use a narrow chisel to remove the wood behind the hole so that the striking latch can work properly (9).

Test the door for operation and make any minor adjustments as necessary. Finally, touch up the patched recesses and any other bare wood with matching paint.

CHANGING DIRECTION

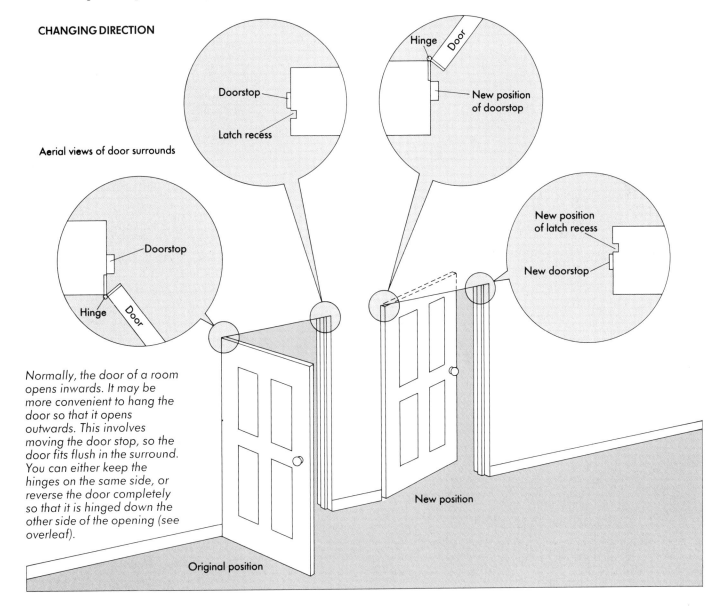

Aerial views of door surrounds

Normally, the door of a room opens inwards. It may be more convenient to hang the door so that it opens outwards. This involves moving the door stop, so the door fits flush in the surround. You can either keep the hinges on the same side, or reverse the door completely so that it is hinged down the other side of the opening (see overleaf).

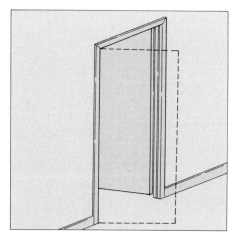

1 When changing the direction a door opens, you must move the door stops as well as hinges and latch.

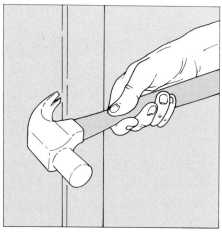

2 Use a claw hammer or chisel and mallet to lever off a door stop which is nailed in place (planted).

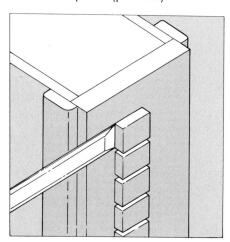

3 If the stop is set into the door frame (rebated) make cuts at the top with a saw then chisel out the wood.

Changing direction

Changing the direction in which a door opens is slighty more complicated than just changing sides. The reason for this is that you have to move the door stops inside the frame as well as the hinges and latch (1).

Before removing and re-hanging a door, check carefully that you will not cause extra problems if it opens the other way. Normally, a door opens inwards. It if it is reversed to open on to a narrow hallway or corridor, it may block the passage, or even become a danger to children and others walking past.

Remove the door from its frame and look at the door stops. There are two common types – planted stops that are simply pinned to the frame and rebated stops that are recesses cut into the frame itself.

To remove a planted stop, simply lever it off with a claw hammer or old chisel, starting at the bottom (2). Once you have pulled off all the stops, sand away any residues of glue and old paint.

To remove a rebated stop, you must first make a series of cuts through one end with a tenon saw and then cut out the chunks with a sharp chisel. When there is enough room for a panel saw, saw away the rest of the stop (3 and 4).

If you decide to change sides as well as direction, you will not have to alter the position of the hinges on the door, but they will have to be fixed to the opposite side of the frame (5). If you simply change direction, you will have to alter the positions of all the door furniture (see **Changing sides,** pages 55–57).

Rehang the door in its new position before fitting a new door stop (6). If necessary, adjust the latch and close the door so that it is flush with the frame. Mark the frame for the position of the striking plate and fit the plate in place.

Keeping the door in its closed position, pin and glue the door stop to the frame – it should butt up against the side of the door. If you cannot reuse the old door stop, you can use new battening instead.

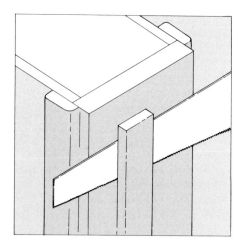

4 When you have chiselled away about 100mm, use a panel saw to cut straight down the door stop.

5 Re-hang the door as described before, adapting hinges and catch as necessary, and filling recesses.

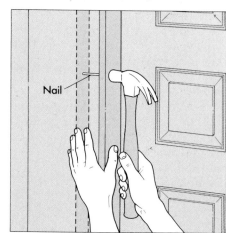
Nail

6 Glue and nail the door stop in position, then fix the latch plate to hold the door closed.

USING THE LOFT

One of the most obvious storage spaces in the average house is the loft – a large area that can accommodate all manner of items, from suitcases to tools and discarded toys. However, lofts should not be abused – they are rarely designed to take a great deal of weight.

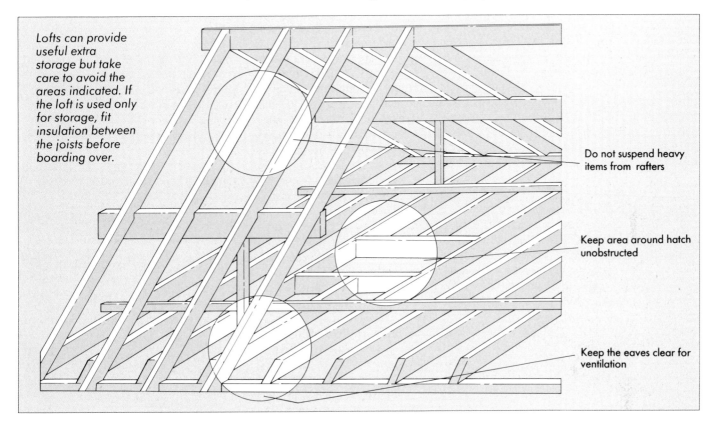

Lofts can provide useful extra storage but take care to avoid the areas indicated. If the loft is used only for storage, fit insulation between the joists before boarding over.

Do not suspend heavy items from rafters

Keep area around hatch unobstructed

Keep the eaves clear for ventilation

In many houses, there is an existing hatch into the loft and the temptation is to hurl things that are essential, but only occasionally used, up into the dark abyss above. What most people do not realize is that the hatch is primarily designed to provide access for plumbers, electricians and other specialists so that they can inspect what the state of play is up in the roof space. Most lofts were not designed for storing household objects – the joists, smaller than flooring joists, are there to support the ceiling below, not trunks full of tin soldiers. Having said that, lofts can obviously be used for storing light items but it is as well to know what you can and cannot do.

● If you want to convert the loft into a major storage area, it will pay to the cover the joists with a flooring material (see pages 62 and 63). A covering will help to distribute the weight evenly over several joists and consequently the risk of the ceiling coming down is reduced. Nevertheless, even if you do introduce flooring, it is always prudent to place heavy items – a laden trunk, perhaps – over a load-bearing wall which supports the joists. That way the weight is transferred to the ground and does not strain the comparatively weak joists.

● It is important to have adequate lighting in a loft when you are up there. This is especially so if you do not put down flooring and have to walk on the joists (for ideas on lighting, see page 64).

● Although it is perfectly possible to get into a loft by precariously heaving yourself off the top of a stepladder, a far better option, especially if you intend to use the loft frequently, is to install a loft ladder (see page 61).

● If you want to use the loft as a living space, you will have to comply with the Building Regulations which specify a number of requirements. The joists have to be strong enough to take the load, a flooring must be added, there must be suitable access, fire precautions must be adhered to, there must be adequate permanent lighting, there must be adequate head height over a given area and there must be adequate natural light via a window. If you want to convert a loft into living space, consult your local Building Inspector first.

● Wiring in a loft should never be tampered with unless you know what you are doing. If there are loose cables, attach them to the sides of the joists with special cable clips.

● Never tamper with the rafters that support the roof – it can even be dangerous to hang things from them as this will add extra strain and, after all, their job is to support the roof.

INSTALLING A LOFT LADDER

A fold-down ladder that leads up to the loft can be a boon, especially if you use the loft frequently or have to take up bulky items. However, before you install the ladder of your choice, you may have to adapt the existing loft hatch so that the ladder will fit into the opening.

Tools and materials: assorted screwdrivers, panel saw or jigsaw, tape measure, pin hammer, spanners, drill and bits, bradawl, 12mm (½in) plywood (for trap and lining), flush hinges (with screws), insulation material, foam draught excluder, auto-latch (push latch), 25mm (1in) panel pins, door stop or quadrant moulding.

Assessing the space

The first thing to do before buying a loft ladder is to assess the space beneath the hatch as well as the hatch opening itself. Measure the height from the top of the ceiling joists to the floor and also take account of the floor space – a person climbing up the ladder laden with a heavy load may need ample clearance from adjacent walls. Also, make a note of the space available in the loft – a hatch that is obstructed by rafters will suit one type of ladder rather than another.

Once you have taken these critical dimensions, you will be in a position to choose a ladder – either a concertina ladder, which takes up less space, or a sliding ladder. However, before you purchase a ladder, do double check that your measurements suit the product.

Converting the hatch

Most houses have convenience hatches which are pushed up and moved to one side to make way. These are not suitable for loft ladders simply because the ladder rests above the opening and it would therefore be impossible to open the hatch up. The answer to this problem is to install a flap-down hatch, hinged on one side; to keep the hatch closed, an auto-latch (the type that you push to open and push to lock) should be installed. An alternative to the auto-latch is a nylon toggle type of catch but these are subject to wear. It is also worth noting that with some types of loft ladder, you may have to enlarge the opening to make room for it. In such cases, it is probably worthwhile calling in a

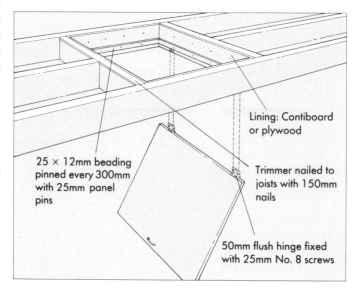

25 × 12mm beading pinned every 300mm with 25mm panel pins

Lining: Contiboard or plywood

Trimmer nailed to joists with 150mm nails

50mm flush hinge fixed with 25mm No. 8 screws

Left: The opening for a loft ladder should be lined, and a hatch fitted with flush hinges and an auto-latch so that it opens downwards.

Right: Loft ladders like this one slide up into the loft. Check that there is enough clearance to store the ladder above the opening before buying.

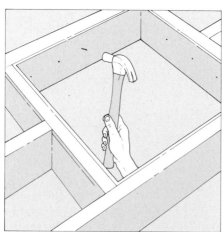

1 To adapt a push-up hatch, remove the beading or architrave then fit a plywood lining if necessary.

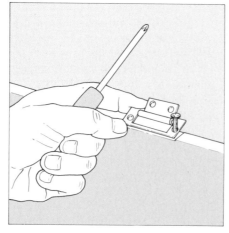

2 Check the panel fits the opening, then fit flush hinges to one edge and a catch to the opposite edge.

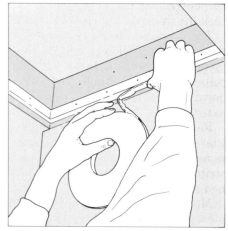

3 Close hatch, mark outline round lining then fit beading and stick self-adhesive foam strip to underside.

60

Fit the flush hinges to the door and then to the opening, making sure that the door aligns with your marks (2). Attach the auto-latch (or nylon clasp) according to the manufacturer's instructions before pinning a moulding or beading around the edges of the opening above the trap door (3). The beading should be pinned about 4mm (⅛in) above the trapdoor. Stick strips of foam draught excluder to the underside of the beading.

To open and close the hatch all you have to do is push up on the auto-latch.

Installing the ladder

Most manufacturers provide fitting instructions for their ladders. Concertina ladders are usually easier to install than sliding ladders because they are lighter.

To fit a concertina ladder, screw the support brackets to the side of the trap opening. With a spirit level, check that the brackets are vertical.

In the closed position, a concertina ladder just rests on a support screwed to the side of the opening opposite the brackets (1). Fix this support in place, making sure that it is at the right height.

Once the ladder has been installed, you can open and close it with a pole provided in the kit (2). Snap on the safety catches before climbing.

carpenter to do the job for you as the task involves cutting joists.

The trapdoor must be hinged to the same joist as the ladder and, ideally, it should be flush with the ceiling. This will enable it to swing down behind the ladder when it is extended.

Remove any architrave or beading that hold the existing trap in place. If necessary, line the opening with strips of plywood which can be pinned and glued in place (1).

Measure up the opening and cut a piece of plywood to fit. While you remain in the loft (make sure there is adequate light), get a friend to hold the trapdoor in place while you mark its position on the lining.

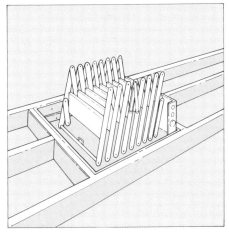

1 When concertina-style ladders are folded away, they sit neatly on top of the hinged loft hatch.

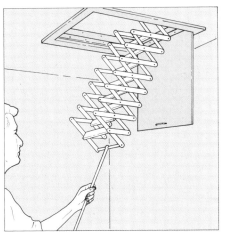

2 Once fitted, the hatch can be opened and the ladder pulled down using the hooked pole supplied.

LOFT FLOORING

Walking about in the loft can be dangerous – it is only too easy to put a foot through the ceiling. The answer is to lay down flooring over the joists. This will not only make the loft safer to move about in but it will also allow you to store things in a more ordered and practical way.

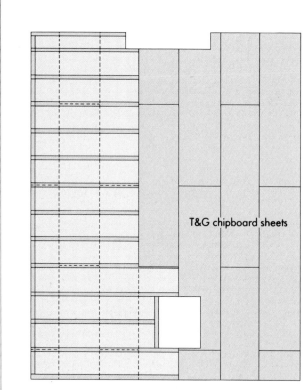

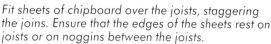

Fit sheets of chipboard over the joists, staggering the joins. Ensure that the edges of the sheets rest on joists or on noggins between the joists.

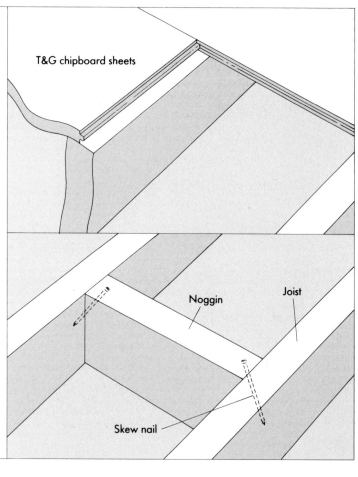

Tools and materials: panel saw, claw hammer, screwdrivers, measuring tape, bolster, flooring material, 50mm (2in) annular ring nails (or 50mm [2in] lost head nails), 100mm × 50mm (4in × 2in) sawn softwood.

There are two common flooring materials that are suitable for a loft – softwood boards or sheets of flooring chipboard. The advantages of chipboard are that it is cheaper and covers a larger area in one go so it is quicker to lay. However, it is bulky and you may have to cut it up to get it into the loft. Boards are easier to handle but they are considerably more expensive. If you decide on sheets, buy flooring grade chipboard with tongued and grooved edges.

There are two common thicknesses – 18mm (²⁄₃in) for joists 400mm (16in) apart and 22mm (⁷⁄₈in) for joists 600mm (2ft) apart. Boards are normally 125mm (5in) wide and again come in two thicknesses – 16mm (⁵⁄₈in) and 19mm (¾in). Both materials can cover over any insulation material between the joists.

Sheet flooring

All the edges of sheet flooring must be supported either on the joists or on special noggins skew-nailed between joists. This is important otherwise the sheets can be dangerous to walk on. Start laying the sheets against a wall or the eaves. Fix them in place with annular nails driven into the joists at 300mm (12in) intervals. Saw sheets to size

as necessary so that the edges are all supported. Butt the sheets tightly together, making sure that the tongues and grooves slot together properly where they meet. Stagger the rows of sheets as you lay them so that the joints do not coincide.

It is a wise precaution to make small access panels over such things as junction boxes which service the lighting system. An access panel can be cut from a sheet and screwed in place to the supporting joists and noggins (extra supports between the joists). When you want to lift up the panel, simply unscrew it.

Boards

Unlike sheets, boards do not have to be supported along all their edges so there is no need to add any noggins

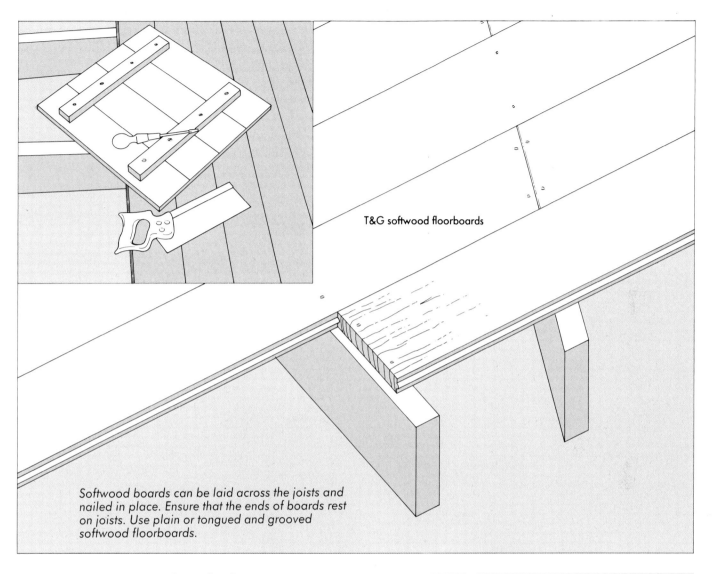

T&G softwood floorboards

Softwood boards can be laid across the joists and nailed in place. Ensure that the ends of boards rest on joists. Use plain or tongued and grooved softwood floorboards.

between joists. However, the ends of the boards must rest on joists, so most of them will have to be sawn to length.

Nail the boards down as you lay them: drive two 50mm (2in) nails through the face of each board where it crosses a joist (1). Make sure that the boards are butted up tight against each other. The easiest way of doing this is to use a stout bolster to lever them together (2). If necessary, make access panels as shown above. Alternatively a series of short boards screwed to the joists will do. Where a cable runs across a joist, cut out a notch for it. Cover the notch – and the cable – with a steel plate screwed in place. The plate will prevent anyone from inadvertently driving a nail into the cable.

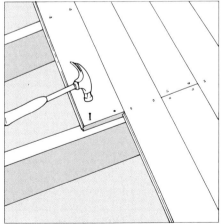

1 Lay the boards, trimming the ends to match joists if necessary. Nail with pairs of nails at each joist. Use a nail punch to knock nails home.

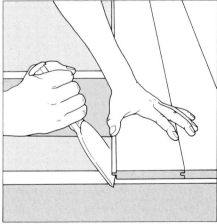

2 For a tightly butted fit with tongued and grooved boards, lever them in place with a bolster wedged under the tongue before nailing in place.

LOFT STORAGE

Cardboard boxes and old suitcases are not very satisfactory when it comes to storing things in the loft. A better option is to use labelled plastic bins or even a storage rack. Bins are a good choice if you have small items to store. By fixing a few hooks or brackets to the rafters, or to a gable wall if you have one, you can free valuable storage space on the floor of the attic. Finally, make sure you have adequate lighting in a loft, especially if it is not floored – it is only too easy to lose your footing in dingy light and wielding a torch is seldom adequate.

Storage rack and bins

These come in a range of colours and sizes and they can stack on top of each other. Be careful when you site bins or racks in the loft – it is best to position them over a load-bearing wall so that strain on the joists is reduced.

Brackets and hooks

Only light items should be suspended from the rafters or else the whole roof may come down. There are any number of hooks and brackets on the market in all shapes and sizes. Screw eyes are useful and they can be fixed to the timbers without the need for a drill and bits.

Lighting

A simple but perfectly acceptable form of lighting is an inspection lamp, the type that is used by car mechanics, on a long lead. This could be plugged into a socket on the floor below and suspended from a hook screwed to the rafters while you are in the loft. Although it is possible to rig up permanent lighting in a loft, this is a job best left to a qualified electrician (see also the companion book, *Electricity and Lighting*).

Left: Well-ventilated lofts are useful for extra clothes storage. Board in the floor and panel in the rafters in the same way, insulating behind the panelling to make the space more habitable.

CONVERTING A FIREPLACE

A blocked off or redundant fireplace can reveal a substantial amount of storage space that can be put to good use, either as a shelving area or as a general deposit. Converting a fireplace is a messy job but the results can be extremely worthwhile, especially in a kitchen or living room.

Tools and materials: club hammer, cold chisel, hacksaw, skip, ground sheets, crowbar, panel saw, spirit level, bolster, drill and bits, pointing trowel, paint brushes, wire brush, hacksaw, screwdrivers, DIY plaster, cellulose filler, cement, builders' sand, assorted nails and screws, exterior grade plywood, ventilator grille, 50mm × 25mm (2in × 1in) battening, preservative.

Before you set about the task of conversion, remove all food products and vulnerable items from the area and while you carry out the project keep all doors to other parts of the house closed.

Chimneys, especially those that have been closed up, produce an immense amount of rubble, so it can be worthwhile hiring a skip for the day (see the Yellow Pages). If you do not want to hire a skip, seek out other alternatives for disposal of the rubbish. It is also worthwhile having the chimney swept.

Once you have prepared the room for the onslaught of dust, use a crowbar to lever away the fireplace (1)—see overleaf. Lever the crowbar against an offcut of timber so that you do not cause unnecessary damage. Fire surrounds can be secured in a number of ways including screws, brackets and lugs. If the fixings prove to be extremely obstinate, cut through them with a hacksaw.

Once you have lifted out the surround, start work on the fireplace itself. First lift out the grate and then tackle the fireback (2). Many

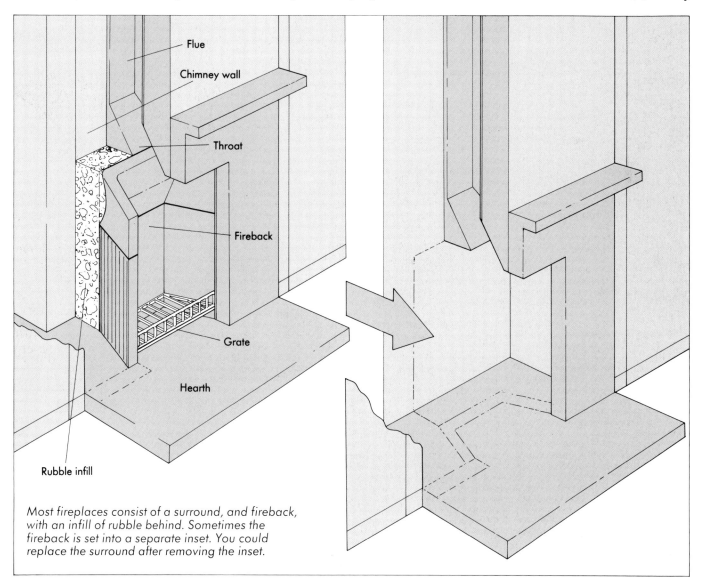

Most fireplaces consist of a surround, and fireback, with an infill of rubble behind. Sometimes the fireback is set into a separate inset. You could replace the surround after removing the inset.

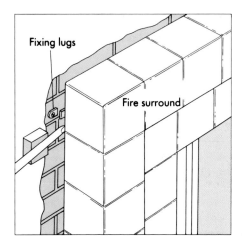

1 Lever the fireplace away from the wall with a crowbar, protecting the plaster with an offcut of wood.

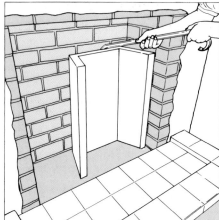

2 Lift out the grate, then lever out the fireback, smashing it to get it out if necessary. Clear away rubble.

3 Knock out any brickwork which is not structural to make a rectangular opening. Clean with a wire brush.

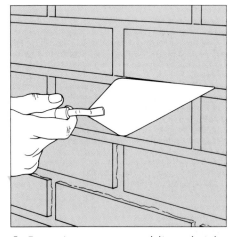

4 Re-point any crumbling brickwork on the back and side walls of the newly exposed opening.

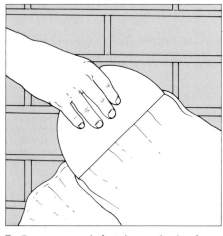

5 For a smooth finish inside the fireplace, apply rendering and plaster, or use a DIY plaster finish.

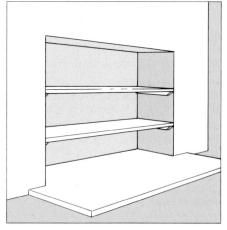

6 Finish the top of the opening and the hearth, then kit it out with shelves fitted on battens.

firebacks come in two halves and in such cases it is best to lever or break out the top half first. Having removed the fireback, you will most likely find a stash of rubble behind it. Shovel this out and dispose of it in your skip.

When you have removed all the rubbish, and cleaned up the brickwork within the surround with a wire brush (3), you will be in a position to smarten up the opening. If the pointing in the back and side walls is weak, repoint the mortar courses using a mixture of five parts builders' (soft) sand to one part cement (4).

With all the rubble removed, you

can start to make good the surround. If you want a completely naked opening, touch up any damage done to the reveals with cellulose filler. If you want a smooth finish to the interior of the fireplace, coat the sides with a thin film of DIY plaster finish (5), following the manufacturer's instructions.

The base of the fireplace may be smooth (for example, concrete), or it may be a hotch-potch of compacted materials. If you are not content with the surface, coat it with a thin mixture of cement and sand.

Soot and plaster may fall down the chimney at some unpredictable stage in the future but precautions

can be taken so that it does not cause any damage. On no account block off the flue completely because this could lead to disastrous damp problems – the flue must have ventilation from the bottom as well as the top. Rig up a 'catch shelf' above the fireplace, using exterior grade plywood supported on preservative treated 50 × 25mm (2 × 1in) battens. Insert a ventilator grille into the centre of the plywood before you fix it in place. The top of the chimney must not be closed off completely – get a builder to cap it off properly.

A good way to finish off the project is to install shelves (6), fitted like alcove shelves (see page 38 and 39).

BASIN VANITORY UNIT

A vanitory unit, built around a basin, can provide storage space for washing and cleaning utensils so that you have everything to hand when you want it.

To complete the look, you could also build a pair of medicine cupboards above and to either side of the basin.

Tools and materials: jigsaw, panel saw, screwdrivers, drill and bits, tape measure, bradawl, post-formed worktop, 15mm (⅝in) melamine faced chipboard, cupboard doors, flush hinges, 12mm (½in) chipboard screws, joint blocks, 32mm (1¼in) No.8 woodscrews, wallplugs, caulking.

Making your own, made-to-measure vanitory unit is a straightforward task once you have assessed exactly what you require. You can adapt this design to suit your needs.

First, you will need to buy off-the-shelf cupboard doors as these will determine the width of the unit. Alternatively you could make your own from plastic- or veneer-faced chipboard, finishing the cut edges with iron-on edging strip or timber moulding. The next thing on your list should be the top of the unit cut from post-formed worktop.

When you have bought all the materials you need, measure out the area of the unit on the floor, making sure that there is equal space on either side of the basin. The width of the unit will equal the combined width of the doors. If you have bought a new basin to sit in the top

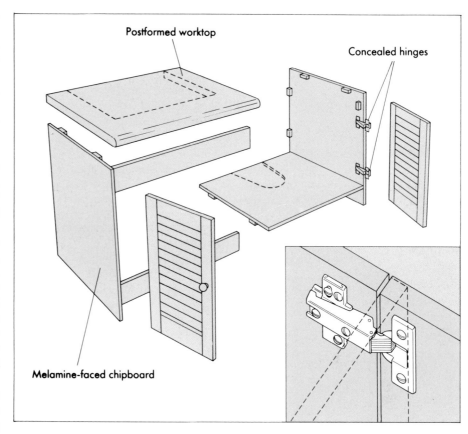

Postformed worktop

Concealed hinges

Melamine-faced chipboard

Above: The unit is made from faced chipboard, topped with a length of postformed worktop. Panels are connected with joint blocks, and the doors are hung on concealed hinges.

Below: Adapt the design according to the size and style of the room: fit a narrower cupboard in a small bathroom, or change the doors or handles to match other furnishings in the room.

of the unit, you can use the sealing ring to mark out the hole that has to be cut in the top (1). If you are building around an existing basin, cut a paper template to size – the hole must be a tight fit, especially if you have a pedestal basin without a lip on it.

Drill a large hole just inside the line you have drawn for the basin aperture and then use a jigsaw to cut out the whole piece (2).

The next stage is to measure up and saw out the side panels along with the shelves, kickboard and fascia (which will all be the same length). If you have a pedestal basin, you will have to cut out slots in the shelves so that they fit round it.

Fix the fascia to the side panels using one joint block at each end – it should be flush with the end of the side panels (3). Next fit the shelves – also flush with the end of the side panels – and lastly attach the kickboard which should be set back from the front by 25mm (1in).

Fix **two** equally spaced joint blocks **down the** inside back edge of **the unit. Push** the unit into place **around the** basin and mark the wall **at the back** for the screw fixings. Remove the unit and drill holes for the screws. Having done this, fix two joint blocks along the top edges of each side panel – these will be used to secure the top.

Hold the top in place so that it surrounds the basin and then manoeuvre in the rest of the unit below it. Fix the unit to the wall through the joint blocks (4) before securing the top to the side panels.

Secure the flush hinges to the doors, following the manufacturer's instructions and then fit the doors to the side panels. The final step is to seal all around the basin, as well as where the unit meets the wall, with caulking (5). If the caulking is uneven, smooth it down with the tip of a wet finger (6) – never be tempted to use a cloth as this will make things worse.

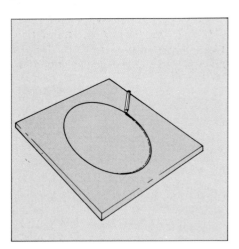

1 For a new, inset basin, use the sealing ring as a guide to mark a cut out into which the basin will fit.

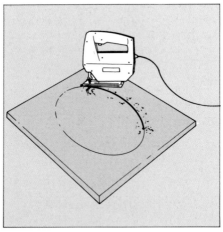

2 To make the cut out, drill a hole within the waste area, insert a jigsaw and cut around the line.

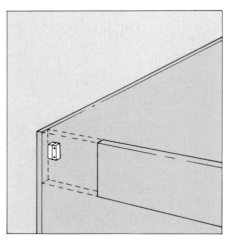

3 Fit the top fascia panel across the side panels, using joint blocks to make firm, true joints.

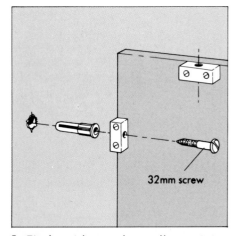

4 Fit the sides to the wall: use joint blocks with chipboard screws and screws and plugs in the wall.

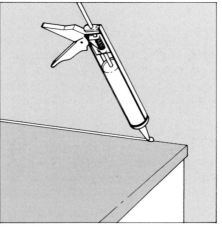

5 Fit the top on the unit with blocks, then seal between top and wall, pushing the tube along the angle.

6 To smooth out the sealant, dip the tip of your finger in water and run it along between worktop and wall.

BUNK BEDS FOR CHILDREN

If your childrens' beds seem to take up every available inch of floor space in their bedroom, why not consider bunk beds? There is a lot to be said for them: they release space for play and storage areas and, besides, children love them. This design is suitable for children of seven years or over.

Tools and materials: jigsaw, tenon saw, tape measure, try square, rasp, drill and bits (including masonry bits), countersink, screwdrivers, socket spanner, medium and fine glass paper, 75mm (3in) masonry loose bolts, joint blocks, 25mm (1in), 38mm (1½in) and 50mm (2in) No.8 woodscrews, 50mm × 50mm (2in × 2in) PAR timber battens, 19mm (¾in) plywood, non-toxic woodwork adhesive, non-toxic paint, non-toxic wood filler.

Although the design can be modified slightly – for example, you may want to make it smaller to fit a mattress size – the dimensions shown in the diagram should not be exceeded as this could jeopardize the stability of the bunks.

Use a jigsaw to cut out the two rectangular side pieces (A and B) from 19mm (¾in) plywood. These have the same outer dimensions although sections will be cut out of A later. Similarly, cut out the end panels, C, making sure that the cuts are square.

The access opening in A should be 1220mm × 762mm (3ft 10in × 2ft 4½in). Mark out the area before you start cutting with a jigsaw. If you want, you can cut out round corners to give the finished article a more friendly appeal.

Cutting out the ladder rails with a jigsaw is one of the most tricky parts of the job (1) – see overleaf. It is easiest to mark out the holes using a card template. When marking out, make sure that all the lines are square to the sides of the panel. The holes should be spaced so they do not coincide with the mattress bases.

Having cut out all the panels, round off all the cut edges with a rasp or file. Then smooth down the grain with glass paper.

The 50mm × 50mm (2in × 2in) support rails have lap joints at each corner – these provide strength to the structure. Saw the side and end rails (D and E) to length and then

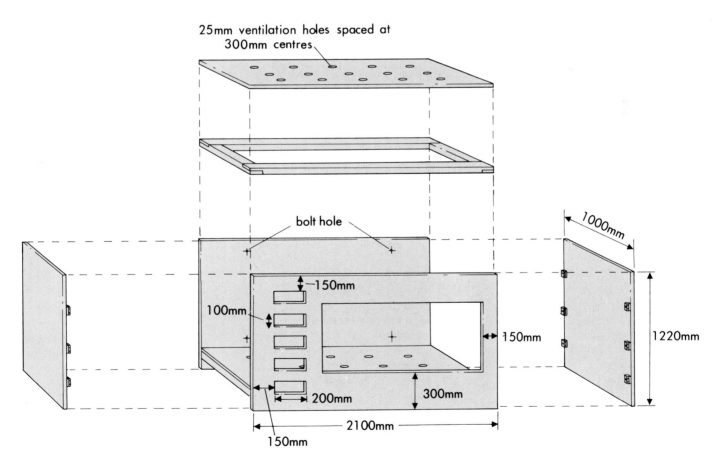

This sturdy bunk bed has a built-in ladder for access to the top level. It is designed to take standard single bed foam mattresses up to 75mm (3in) thick. For extra stability, the back panel is bolted to a solid wall.

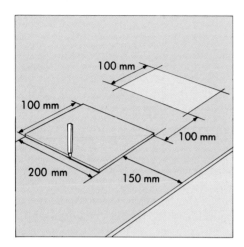

1 Start by cutting out the panels. Cut an opening in the front. Mark holes for ladder using a card template.

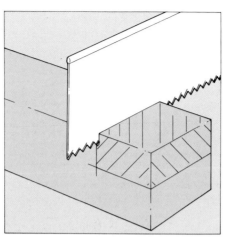

2 Cut battens for mattress supports, and make two frames, cutting lap joints at corners using a tenon saw.

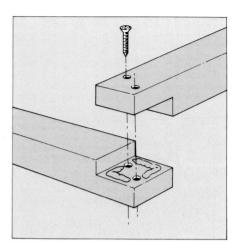

3 Apply wood glue to each side of the halving joint, then screw each joint with two woodscrews.

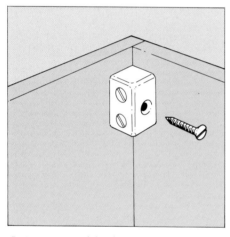

4 Use joint blocks to join the end panels to the side panels, fitting three blocks down each corner.

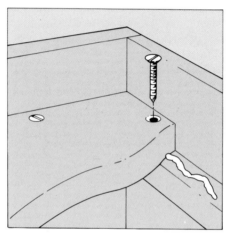

5 Fix the support rails to the panels, then glue and screw the mattress bases to the rails.

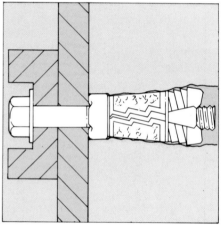

6 The bolts should slot through the mattress support and the side panel into the wall.

cut out halving joints using a tenon saw (2). Apply adhesive to the mating surfaces of each joint before fixing them with pairs of countersunk 38mm (1½in) screws (3).

Join the side (A and B) and end (C) panels together with joint blocks – so that the end panels are within the sides. Use 25mm (1in) screws to fix three joint blocks per corner (4). For this stage you will almost certainly need an assistant to hold things steady for you.

Mark the position of the support rails on the inside of the 'box' structure – the top rail should be flush with the top edge of the access opening and the bottom rail should be 100mm (4in) up from the base of the unit. Drill countersunk clearance holes through the side and end panels at 300mm (1ft) centres and fix the rails in place with adhesive and 50mm (2in) screws.

The next stage is to cut out and secure the mattress bases to the support rails. Cut out the bases from sheets of 19mm (⅔in) plywood drilled at 150mm (6in) centres with a 10mm (⅜in) bit. Drill through countersunk clearance holes along the edges every 350mm (1ft 2in). Fix the bases to the supports with adhesive and 38mm (1½in) woodscrews (5).

The bunk bed assembly must be anchored to a solid wall along at least one side panel with masonry bolts. You may need spacers, the thickness of the skirting board, between the plywood and the wall. Drill counterbored clearance holes for the bolts through the upper support batten and the plywood and then position the unit against the wall and mark for the holes. Drill out the holes with a masonry bit. Insert the anchors in the holes and bolt through the batten, side panel and spacer into the anchors. Tighten the bolts up with a socket or box spanner (6).

Fill over all the screw heads, flush with the surface, and finish with non-toxic paint.

PART 3

TOOLS, TECHNIQUES AND MATERIALS

The final section shows a range of useful tools and materials, with suggestions for what to use where. Some of the items covered are:

- Tools for measuring and marking, and cutting.

- Chisels, hammers and nails, screws and screwdrivers, drills and bits.

- Tools and materials for a perfect finish.

- Timbers and boards and how to choose and use them.

- A range of mouldings that will provide a neat professional finish.

- A look at the choices available in doors and knobs, hinges and hooks.

MEASURING AND MARKING TOOLS

Accurate measuring and marking is especially important when doing woodwork. The professional's rule is to measure twice, then mark, then double check. Inaccuracies may lead, at best, to a lot of time spent in adaption later, or at worst may necessitate buying more timber. Tools need to be looked after with care and stored in a dry place or they may become faulty. Check their accuracy regularly.

Measuring tools

Retractable steel tape Available with metric measurements only or with metric and imperial, this is an accurate (usually to within 1mm) and widely used measuring tool. A 3m (10ft) rule is generally the most useful length and a thumb lock and top sight are both handy.

Metre rule These rigid rules can be of wood, metal or plastic and give metric or imperial measurements. Lengths longer than 1m (3ft) cannot be measured accurately.

Folding rule Traditionally made of boxwood, folding rules are more portable than straight rules. They are also available in metal and plastic. Lengths are from 300mm (12in) to 2m (6ft 6in) The most commonly used length is 120cm (4ft).

For measuring angles

Try square Used for marking square ends on a length of wood, for marking other right angles and for checking their accuracy, a try square has a steel blade and a wood, steel or plastic stock and both internal and external edges form a 90° angle. They come in sizes from 150mm (6in) to 300mm (12in).

Combination square This can be used for measuring and checking right angles and 45° mitres; it can also check the depth of mortises.

Mitre block Used for making mitres across small pieces of wood, a mitre block is L-shaped and has two slots, one at 45° and one at 90°. The wood is placed in the L and one of the slots is used to guide the saw.

Marking tools

Carpenter's pencil A chisel-shaped pencil is easier to use against a rule than an ordinary pencil but the latter is adequate for marking.

Marking knife A special marking knife with an angled steel blade is more accurate than a pencil.

Marking gauge Used to mark lines parallel to the edge or end of timber or board, a marking gauge has a steel point close to the end of the stem and a sliding stock that can be locked with a screw on the side at

1. Marking gauge, 2. Combination gauge, 3. Spirit level, 4. Carpenter's pencil, 5. Metre rule, 6. Try square, 7. Folding rule, 8. Marking knife, 9. Plumb bob, 10. Steel tape, 11. Combination square.

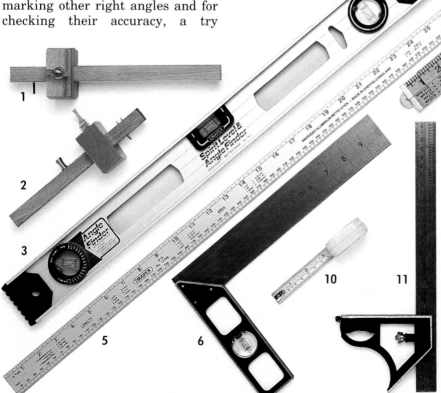

the required distance from the point.

Mortise gauge This has two pins, one of which can be moved up and down then set to the required spacing for marking mortises and tenons.

Combination gauge This combines both the above operations.

Levelling tools

Spirit level Used to check that a surface is level, the longer the spirit level the more accurate it will be over a distance. Lengths range from 75mm (3in) to 2m (6ft 6in).

Plumb bob A tool used for accurate alignment of verticals, this consists of a brass or steel weight which is attached to a line and hung from a pin or nail.

HOLDING DEVICES

A work bench and a vice or cramps to hold the work steady are essential for many woodworking tasks. If you can find the space in a garage, garden shed, or elsewhere to create a working area with a fixed bench and racks and shelves for tools and materials this is ideal. If you are short of space, a folding bench can go where the work is. Do not forget safety equipment is part of your toolkit.

Portable workbench

This makes working on the spot much easier and it is useful where space is limited. This freestanding folding bench (below) incorporates vice jaws and acts as a sawhorse. Bench height is 765mm (30in), sawhorse height 590mm (23in).

Bench hook

This is an easily fashioned holding device made from a piece of timber approximately 150mm (6in) wide and 225mm (9in) long with a block attached at each end on opposite sides.

Vices and cramps

Woodworkers vice A vice that can be clamped on to the bench to hold timber still when being sawn, drilled or prepared in any other way is important both from a safety and accuracy angle.
G-cramp A G-shaped tool used for securing objects to the bench. A crab cramp does the same job.
Quick action cramp In this cramp the serrated stem allows the jaw width to be quickly adjusted.
Corner cramp Useful for ensuring firm, true corners on such things as picture frames, this is a cramp for holding mitred corners.

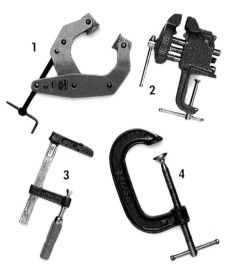

1. Crab cramp, 2. Multi-purpose vice, 3. Quick action cramp, 4. G-cramp.

Tool Storage

Carrying boxes These are barn-shaped metal boxes with a lift-off shelf at the top and space for tools in the base.
Cantilevered metal box Larger ones have four storage containers in the top which open out to the sides when the box is opened, allowing you to see all the contents at once.
Plastic carrying containers These have a shelf in the top with holes through which you slot the tools, a shelf for small items and two deep trays at the bottom.
Bags The traditional carpenter's bag will carry a variety of tools.

For smaller items

Transparent, plastic drawer boxes These small containers are good for storing fixings and drill bits separately.
Plastic stacking bins These will take larger quantities of accessories than drawer boxes.
Handled plastic tray These open boxes with a central division and handle are also useful for carrying small quantities of tools.

Storage in the workshop

Use jam jars on a shallow shelf to hold screws and nails of different sizes. A second layer can be included by screwing lids to the underneath of the shelf.

Perforated hardboard fixed to the wall and used with tool hanging clips or wire hooks is a good way of storing hand tools.

Use nails or dowels fixed into battens and positioned to hang larger tools like saws and hammers. If you paint a simple silhouette behind each tool's position you will instantly know whether one has been borrowed!

Make a rack with holes drilled to the size of the blades of chisels, files and screwdrivers so that they will neatly slot through, leaving the handles upright and above.

Safety equipment

Goggles Use protective goggles when using a circular saw, breaking up concrete or stone, drilling metal, electric welding or any situation when dust or bits may be flying about.
Mask A mask will protect throat and lungs when you are working with dangerous chemicals and adhesives or with cement, brick, or plaster or sanding wood and creating fine dust.
Ear muffs Most muffs are designed to protect from noise levels between 90 and 110 decibels.

SAFETY TIPS
- Keep tools sharp
- Stop work when you are tired
- Do not cut corners
- Mend tools immediately
- Keep your body and hands out of the line of cut when sawing and keep your fingers behind the blade of a cutting knife

CUTTING TOOLS

The main cutting tools used in DIY, especially for woodwork, are saws. There are four main types of wood saw: rip saws for cutting along the grain of the wood; cross-cut saws for cutting across the grain; panel saws for general sawing and for use on man-made boards; and those saws used for cutting curves and special shapes. There are also special saws for metal work, and two main types of power saw. A saw is sold in a point size – this is the number of saw teeth, plus one, per 25mm (1in). So a 10-point saw has nine teeth every 25mm (1in). Small, close-set teeth provide a finer but slower cut than larger teeth. A trimming knife and a pair of scissors are the other useful cutting tools.

Saws for straight cuts

Panel saw Designed for cutting panels of manmade board such as chipboard and ply as well as planks. This is an all-round hand saw which will cut both with and across the grain, although more slowly than the specially designed larger toothed saws below.
Rip saw Designed for cutting along the grain of the timber.
Cross-cut saw Designed to cut across the grain of timber.
Tenon saw Used for making most woodworking joints (as well as cutting tenons) and for cutting accurate angles like mitres, in conjunction with a mitre box.

Special purpose saws

Narrow blades can be removed and replaced as soon as they lose their sharpness.
Coping saw Designed to cut in any direction on the forward stroke.
Fret saw ideal for cutting very tight curves in thin woods like plywood, plus other materials such as plastic and glass fibre.
Keyhole or pad saw Used for cutting a keyhole or making an enclosed cut in a large panel where the handle would render a coping saw inoperable.
Hacksaw Basic saw for cutting metal and plastic.
Junior hacksaw Useful in confined spaces because it is smaller than the regular hacksaw.
Circular saw This is ideal for straight cutting of timber, manmade boards including laminated boards and plastic, metal, masonry and ceramic tiles but is not suitable for cutting tight curves. **Safety point:** fit upper and lower blade guards before using a circular saw.
Jigsaw This is the power saw for cutting curves and enclosed cut-out shapes to fit a built-in hob or sink for instance. Different blades to suit different materials are also available.
Trimming and marking knife Used for scoring lines and for trimming vinyl, carpet, polystyrene etc.

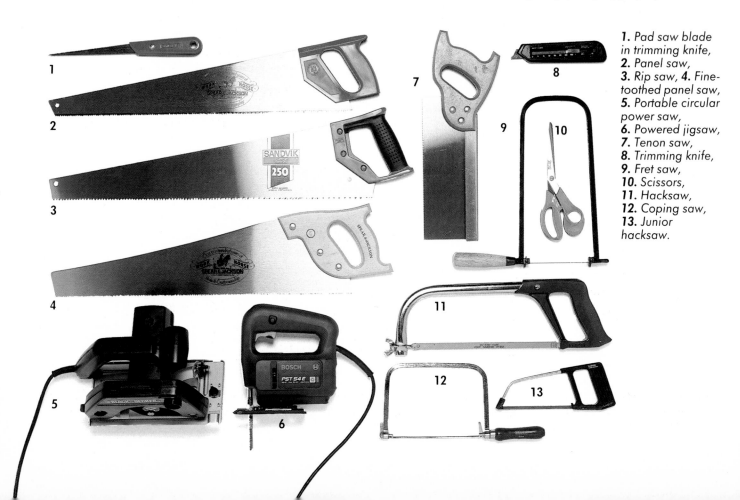

1. Pad saw blade in trimming knife, *2.* Panel saw, *3.* Rip saw, *4.* Fine-toothed panel saw, *5.* Portable circular power saw, *6.* Powered jigsaw, *7.* Tenon saw, *8.* Trimming knife, *9.* Fret saw, *10.* Scissors, *11.* Hacksaw, *12.* Coping saw, *13.* Junior hacksaw.

74

MAKING STRAIGHT CUTS

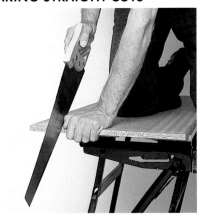

1. Draw the saw towards you at a shallow angle to start a cut. Use your thumb as guide.

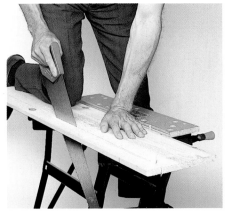

2. When nearing the end on a long cut wedge the cut open with scrap timber and support the wood.

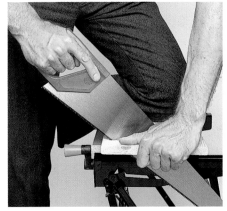

3. When ending a cut across the grain support the overhanging end to avoid splitting the wood.

CUTTING CURVES

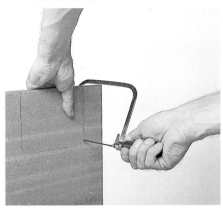

1. Saw with the teeth downwards, only angling it to avoid obstructions such as an edge or corner.

2. Finish by cutting with the blade facing upwards. Check at each point that the blade is not twisted.

USING A CIRCULAR SAW

A rip guide helps you to cut at a fixed distance from the edge of the timber.

MAKING HOLES

Thread the blade through pre-drilled hole with teeth facing downwards. Cut on the downward stroke.

Drill holes to thread the pad saw through, then apply pressure and cut on the backward stroke.

USING A JIGSAW

Drill a hole at each corner of a cut-out for a smoother finish than the saw will achieve.

CHISELS

These are used for making joints, paring wood and cutting recesses to take fittings such as hinges. They are also useful for cutting away areas of rotting woodwork. Chisels have a flat steel blade with a cutting edge on the end. The handles can be of wood, in which case it is important when necessary to tap the handle to use a wood mallet, or they can be of tough plastic, when an ordinary hammer will suffice. New chisels are not sharpened and need honing on an oilstone before they can be used.

Types of chisel

When buying a chisel avoid any that are thin at the blade shoulder (a chisel's weakest point). Look for those with a slight taper from shoulder to blade end.

Bevel-edge chisel This is the most common type of chisel. It has sloping sides which mean that it can be used in confined spaces to undercut or cut sideways into the corner of an acute angle. Sizes from 6mm (⅜in) to 38mm (1½in).

Firmer chisel The sides of this chisel are straight rather than bevel-edged and it is therefore considered a stronger tool. However, strength also comes from the steel used and the design of the blade. This chisel is

Sharpening a chisel

Apart from sharpening when new, chisels need checking regularly before use. A blunt chisel is difficult to use and produces poor results.

Use a medium or fine oilstone to sharpen and apply light oil or paraffin, which is cleaner, to the surface. Remove the surplus with a rag. Hold the handle of the chisel in one hand and steady the blade with the other, keeping the chisel, bevel side down, at an angle of 25° for the bevel, then at 30° for honing. If the angle is increased the chisel becomes harder to use, if it is decreased it will blunt rapidly. Use a honing guide to ensure the correct angle (1).

When a wire edge starts to form turn the blade over and, keeping the blade flat on the surface, rub it over the stone. Rub the back of the blade over the stone in a side-to-side movement (2). Repeat this action until the sliver of steel on the tip of the chisel has disappeared.

If a blade is damaged, with nicks in it, or has rounded corners it will need regrinding. This is hard work and it is best to take it to a local DIY shop, which can probably arrange for this to be done.

For safety and to protect blades, use a well-fitting blade guard on chisels when not in use.

Above: 1, 2 and 3. Paring chisels in three different widths, 4. Bevel-edge chisel, 5. Firmer chisel, 6. Bolster chisel for heavier work.

1 Use a honing guide to hold the bevelled side of the chisel at the correct angle – in this case, 30°.

2 Rub the back of the chisel from side to side to remove the wire edge created by honing.

good for making partition frames or fencing or for cutting out notches for pipes running over joists.

Mortise chisel This is the strongest chisel of all. It has a thicker blade and is used for cutting the mortise of a mortise and tenon joint. It is de-signed for striking with a mallet and for levering.

Paring chisel This can be bevel-edged or straight-sided but the blade is long and thin. It is useful for cutting out deep holes or paring long slots in wood such as those needed for bookcase housings.

Bolster chisel Apart from cutting masonry, this chisel can be used for a number of levering jobs such as taking up floorboards. Lengths range from 175mm to 190mm (7 to 7½in).

Using chisels

Cutting a halving joint Mark out the width lines across the top of the timber, and width and depth lines down the sides. Make a saw cut to the waste side of each width line and down to the depth line (1).

Place securely in a vice, making sure the timber is horizontal. Use the chisel pointing slightly upwards and chisel out from one side to the centre, then the other (2). Finally, use the chisel horizontally to shave off the remaining fibres. Clean out corners.

Cutting a mortise Mark out the area of the mortise. Use the correct width chisel and drive it into the centre of the waste area, using a mallet or hammer for a wood or plastic handle respectively, to a depth of about 5mm (¼in) (3). Make successive cuts either side of this to within 3mm (⅛in) of each end and remove waste.

Mark the final depth on the chisel with tape and gradually work down through the wood to this depth (4). Clean up the edges with a vertically held chisel. Continually check fit with the other half of the joint.

Paring wood vertically Mark the curve required on your wood and cut off the corners with a tenon saw (5).

Pressing down with the thumb, cut towards the marked line, taking off finer and finer shavings (6).

1 Use a tenon saw to make clean cuts on each side of halving joint.

2 Chisel away the waste, working in from each side of the timber.

3 Make a series of vertical cuts into a mortise, with the chisel vertical.

4 Remove the waste, using tape as a depth guide on the chisel.

5 Trim the end of a piece of timber with a tenon saw.

6 Use a paring chisel, held vertical-ly, to pare away the waste.

HAMMERS AND NAILS

Most hammers have a head of heat-treated steel that makes the striking face hard enough for constantly knocking in nails yet not so brittle that it could shatter. It is the weight of this head that a hammer is sold by.

The two basic woodworking hammers are claw and cross-pein hammers, but there are other specialist hammers from small headed ones for tapping in panel pins to those used for breaking up concrete. It pays to buy the best you can afford.

Hammering tools

Claw hammer Check when buying that the claw V is tapered enough to be suitable for pulling out small panel pins as well as larger nails. The shaft can be of wood, glass fibre, or steel (the strongest) and if made of the latter will have a handle covered with a shock-absorbing grip. If this becomes slippery in hot weather run the sleeve under the cold tap. Weights most common are 450g (16oz), 510g (18oz) and 570g (20oz).

Cross-pein hammer Designed for general carpentry work, the end of the head, the pein, is tapered rather than claw-shaped. This is designed for starting off pins and tacks that are held between the fingers, or for getting into awkward corners. The shaft is made of wood and the heaviest head weight is 450g (16oz).

Pin hammer This is a slimmer version of the cross-pein hammer and is used for delicate work where a heavier hammer could bend the pin. Head weights go up to 110g (4oz).

Mallet A wooden carpenter's mallet is used for driving chisels when cutting joints. Heads come in widths up to 150mm (6in).

Pin push Used for driving thin pins without a hammer, a pin push is used when fixing thin board to a frame. The magnetized end tube takes the pin; the push is then held in place and driven in by pumping the spring-loaded handle.

Nail punch This is a handy tool designed for use with a hammer to drive headless nails or panel pins just below the surface of timber. You can then fill the hole, making the fixing invisible. You can also use a nail punch for the final part of driving in a nail to avoid marking the surface. Tip diameters are from 0.5mm to 4.5mm (about $\frac{1}{50}$ in to $\frac{1}{5}$ in). Use a size smaller than the nail head to avoid enlarging the hole.

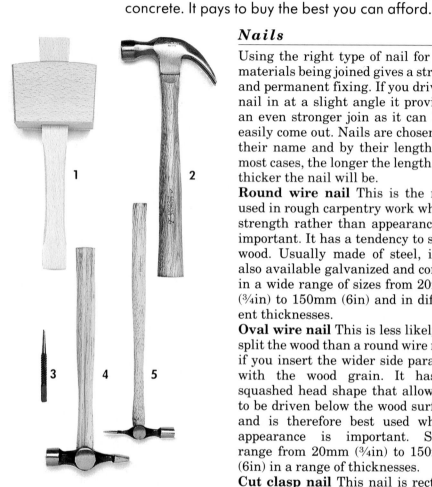

1. Wooden mallet, 2. Claw hammer,
3. Nail punch, 4. Cross-pein hammer,
5. Pin hammer.

Removing nails

Crow (wrecking) bar The large, curved, claw-shaped end is designed for lifting large nails such as floorboards nails and the flattened end can be used to prise up the boards, the length providing good leverage.

Carpenter's pincers The rounded and polished head of these pincers is designed for pulling out nails and tacks. They come in sizes from 150mm (6in) to 250mm (10in).

Claw hammer The back of a claw hammer is designed for lifting nails, and is convenient to use when a nail bends or goes in at an angle.

Nails

Using the right type of nail for the materials being joined gives a strong and permanent fixing. If you drive a nail in at a slight angle it provides an even stronger join as it can less easily come out. Nails are chosen by their name and by their length. In most cases, the longer the length the thicker the nail will be.

Round wire nail This is the nail used in rough carpentry work where strength rather than appearance is important. It has a tendency to split wood. Usually made of steel, it is also available galvanized and comes in a wide range of sizes from 20mm (¾in) to 150mm (6in) and in different thicknesses.

Oval wire nail This is less likely to split the wood than a round wire nail if you insert the wider side parallel with the wood grain. It has a squashed head shape that allows it to be driven below the wood surface and is therefore best used where appearance is important. Sizes range from 20mm (¾in) to 150mm (6in) in a range of thicknesses.

Cut clasp nail This nail is rectangular in shape, making it extra strong and difficult to remove. It is used for fixing wood to masonry and is inserted in already drilled, slightly smaller holes. It comes in lengths from 50mm (2in) to 100mm (4in).

Cut floor brad This nail has an L-shaped head and is designed for fixing floorboards to joists. The head shape makes them difficult to start but they are unlikely to split the wood. Made of black iron or steel, they are available in three lengths, 50mm (2in), 60mm (2⅜in) and 65mm (2½in).

Panel pin This small, slim nail is used to fix mouldings, to reinforce glued joints, for cabinet making and for picture frames. The pin head can be easily punched in. Made of brass, copper, galvanized and mild steel they come in lengths from 12mm (½in) to 50mm (2in).

Veneer pin This is similar to a panel pin but has a thinner shank. It is used for fixing small mouldings and veneers and in cabinet making. Made of brass or steel it comes in lengths from 12mm (½in) to 25mm (1in).

Hardboard nail Used for fixing hardboard or thin plywood, this nail has a diamond-shaped head that is easily driven below the surface. Hardboard nails, which do not have a very strong grip, come with a copper finish or in steel in lengths from 20mm (¾in) to 25mm (1in).

Plasterboard nail This nail, which is not widely available, has a jagged

1. 50mm round wire nail, 2. 25mm panel pin, 3. 15mm veneer pin, 4. Cut-floor brad, 5. 25mm oval wire nail, 6. 20mm hardboard nail, 7. Cut-clasp nail, 8. 25mm round wire nail, 9 Wiggle nail.

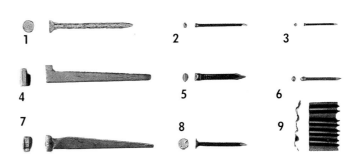

shank that stops the nail from being pulled out. Used for fixing plasterboard or other manmade boards, it comes in galvanized or mild steel and in 30mm (1⅛in) or 35mm (1⅜in) lengths.

Ringed shank nail The rings around the shank of this nail also help to prevent it being pulled out.

Used for fixing manmade boards, it comes in mild steel in lengths from 20mm (¾in) to 100mm (4in).

Wiggle nail This corrugated mild steel fastener is used in frame construction, for mitred and butt joints. It does not provide a very strong fixing. It comes in sizes from 12mm (½in) to 25mm (1in).

Tips on using hammers and nails

Start off a nail by tapping gently then grip the hammer near to the end and, keeping your eyes on the nail, strike the head cleanly with a firm stroke from the elbow, keeping the wrist rigid.

Hold a short nail between finger and thumb and tap it gently with the chisel-shaped end of a cross-pein hammer until the nail will stand on its own (1). Then use the hammer face to drive it in.

When working with very small pins, first push the head through a small rectangle of plastic or card and use this to hold the nail upright (2). Just before nailing home pull the polythene away. Use a piece of cardboard in the same way as the polythene on larger nails to avoid damage to the wood surface.

To avoid splitting wood, stagger nail positions and for strength drive nails home at a slight angle (3).

To avoid damaging the surface from which a nail is being removed, slide a slim scrap of wood beneath the hammer head and lever on this (4).

When using pincers to remove a nail, use a series of short sharp tugs rather than one long one as this can leave a larger and misshapen hole.

1 Start a nail with a cross pein.

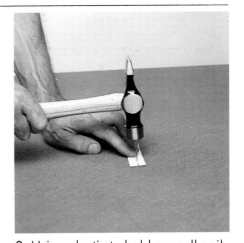

2 Using plastic to hold a small nail.

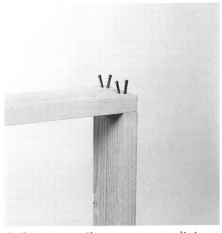

3 Stagger nails to prevent splitting.

4 Use offcut to protect the surface.

SCREWDRIVERS AND SCREWS

Choose screws and screwdrivers to suit the type of work you are doing. Whether you are screwing heavy timber to the wall for a built-in unit, or simply fixing a hook to the back of a door, the right tools will make the job easier. The handle of a screwdriver must be comfortable to grip, particularly if you have a lot of work to do. When working with faced sheet materials, screw caps give a neat finish.

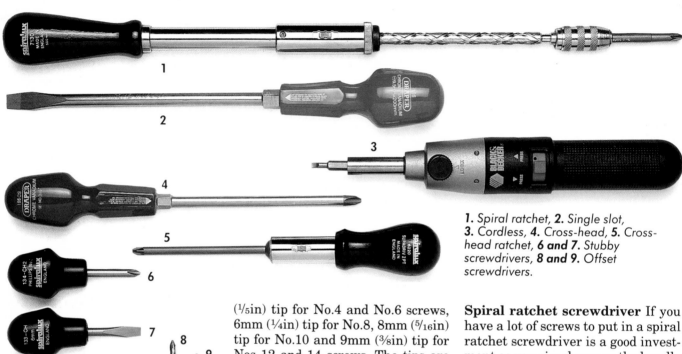

1. Spiral ratchet, 2. Single slot, 3. Cordless, 4. Cross-head, 5. Cross-head ratchet, 6 and 7. Stubby screwdrivers, 8 and 9. Offset screwdrivers.

Screwdrivers

A screwdriver is one of the most essential tools. Most people will need a single slot screwdriver in three or four sizes to fit a range of single-slot screws, plus cross-head screwdrivers to match Phillips and Posidriv screws. You can buy sets of screwdriver bits that fit one handle. A ratchet screwdriver makes the action easier and a pump action screwdriver speeds up work when you are fixing or undoing a number of screws. Many electric drills can be used with special screwdriver bits and cordless screwdrivers are also now available that come with a selection of bits.

Single-slot screwdriver These come in a number of sizes to fit the range of single-slot screws – 5mm (⅕in) tip for No.4 and No.6 screws, 6mm (¼in) tip for No.8, 8mm (⁵⁄₁₆in) tip for No.10 and 9mm (⅜in) tip for Nos 12 and 14 screws. The tips are chisel shaped; when buying, pick one that has clean, sharp corners. The blades are generally longer as the blade size increases.

Cross-head screwdriver There are a number of different types of cross-head screw and to get a good grip it is best to match up the screwdriver; this also ensures that the screw heads will not get damaged. Supadriv screwdrivers will also drive Pozidriv screws. These screwdrivers are available in three sizes; No.1 point fits screw gauges 1–4, No.2 sizes 5–10 and No.3 gauges over 10.

Stubby screwdriver These are ideal when you are working in a confined space. They come in both single-slot and cross-head styles.

Ratchet screwdriver These make driving in screws easier as they allow you to fit or remove a screw without taking the head out of the slot in the screw. Available in both single-slot and cross-head styles, a control changes the action from clockwise to anticlockwise and they can also be used fixed.

Spiral ratchet screwdriver If you have a lot of screws to put in a spiral ratchet screwdriver is a good investment as you simply pump the handle and the spiral grooves do the work. The blades or bits can be changed to suit the type of screw.

Offset screwdriver The double ended right-angle shape provides extra leverage when you have to position a screw in an inaccessible spot.

Impact driver This is a useful tool for freeing stuck screws and nuts. Position the driver on the screw head and tap with a hammer.

Cordless screwdriver These are single-speed and come with forward and reverse action for inserting and removing screws.

Screws

Timbers joined together with screws are more secure than those attached with nails or glue because the spiral shape and turning action draw the two components together. The use of screws also means that an item can be dismantled much more easily.

The screw size is determined by the diameter of the screw shank (gauge) and the length is the measurement from head to thread tip.

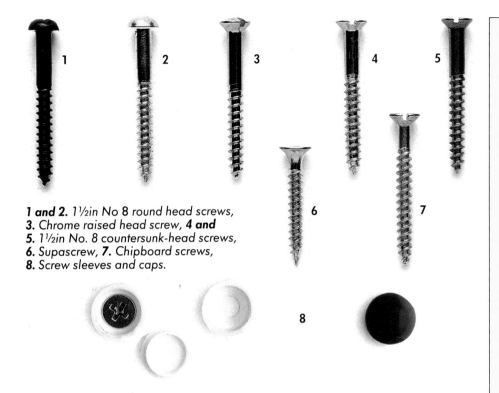

1 and 2. 1½in No 8 round head screws,
3. Chrome raised head screw, *4 and*
5. 1½in No. 8 countersunk-head screws,
6. Supascrew, *7.* Chipboard screws,
8. Screw sleeves and caps.

Each gauge of screw is available in a number of different lengths.

In order to stop the wood splitting you should first make a pilot hole slightly smaller than the screw gauge. This will allow the screw to bite as it is driven home. A shorter hole of the screw gauge size and shank length is needed to take the smooth shank of the screw and, if you are using flat countersunk-head screws, you will need to make a third shallow hole with a countersinking bit to take the screw head.

Single-slot countersunk-head screw This is the general woodworking screw. The head is designed to lie flush with or just below the wood surface. This style comes in plain mild steel or a range of corrosion-resistant finishes and in lengths from 6mm (¼in) to 150mm (6in) and gauges from 0–20.

Cross-head countersunk-head screw This can be used in the same situations as a single-slot screw but because of the slot shape a cross-head screw can be positioned on the end of a matching screwdriver, so it easier to use in confined spaces.

Roundhead screw These are usually used for attaching metal fittings to wood. Made of steel or brass, the lengths range from 6mm (¼in) to 75mm (3in) and gauges from 0–14. For a neat finish, align the slots on the screws.

Raised countersunk-head screw This screw is designed to be countersunk to its rim and can also be used with a screw cup. It comes in steel or brass and in lengths from 9.5mm (⅜in) to 50mm (2in) and more, and gauges from 4–10.

Chipboard and quick drive screw This design is specially suitable for use with manmade boards and softwoods. It comes in lengths from 13mm (½in) to around 75mm (3in) and in gauges from 4–12.

Double-ended screw This is a screw with no head but instead a screw thread at each end. It is made to provide an invisible fixing when screwing two wooden items together. Lengths are from 25–50mm (1–2in); gauges from 6–12.

Dome-headed screw This has a separate screw-in head and can be used for a decorative fixing for mirrors, panels and splashbacks. When fixing mirrors be careful not to over-tighten the screw as this can crack the glass.

TIPS ON USING SCREWDRIVERS AND SCREWS

• Use the correct size of screwdriver for the screw.
• Use a bradawl to make a starting hole for screws up to No.6 gauge, and a drill bit for larger screws.
• Always position the blade of the screwdriver square in the screw slot and use it this way.
• Screws positioned close to the edge of wood can cause it to split. Always drill pilot holes to avoid this.
• Do not try to drive the complete length of a screw larger than gauge 7 into a small pilot hole. Instead, make a second shorter hole the size of the screw to take the shank.
• A lubricated screw is easier to fit and remove and is less likely to corrode. Use a light covering of wax or grease.
• Softwoods require smaller pilot holes than hardwood.
• Never use screwdrivers for other jobs such as opening tins of paint as this will damage the blade.
• Sharpen a screwdriver with a grindstone. Aim to get good sharp corners and taper evenly to the edge on both sides.
• If a screw has a damaged slot use the longest screwdriver you have to release it – this will provide the most force.
• A paint-fixed screw can be released by brushing with paint stripper first to loosen the paint. Alternatively, tapping the end of the screwdriver lightly with a hammer will often break the paint seal.
• To loosen a seized screw turn once as if screwing in tighter before unscrewing; this often loosens it. Alternatively, use an impact driver to free seized screws (see opposite).

DRILLS AND BITS

Hand drills are slow and easy to control and are therefore the sensible choice when very precise holes are required in wood or metal. However, when you are making holes in masonry, an electric drill will do the job much more easily. The bit (the part that actually drills the hole) is chosen by size, the material it is to be used on and the type of hole. Hand drills can only be used with a small range of bits while electric drills come with a wider range, making them suitable for drilling holes in a much larger variety of materials. For tough masonry a hammer drill is necessary.

Drills and braces

Hand drill This has a handle on a gear wheel which is turned to twist the bit into the material. It will take drill bits up to 8mm (5/16in) in diameter.

Hand brace For larger holes in wood use a hand brace which has a U-shaped rotating frame.

Breast drill This is similar to a hand drill but larger and can be used to make holes in metal and masonry as well as wood.

Push drill Useful for making small holes for screws in wood, it works like a spiral ratchet screwdriver. It takes special small bits from 2mm to 4.4mm (1/16 to 3/16in) in size.

Cordless drill These are suitable for drilling a variety of thicknesses of wood, steel and brick.

Electric drill Two-speed or variable-speed drills are more flexible than those with one speed only. A hammer action drill is useful for drilling hard materials and a reverse switch is also included on some models. Many attachments and accessories are available.

For boring holes

Bradawl This small hand tool is twisted back and forth to make a starting hole for a screw.

Gimlet This hole-boring tool is used by twisting round and round.

Bits

Twist drill bits The most widely used bits for drilling holes, they come in sizes up to around 13mm (½in) in diameter.

Dowel bit These are for making flat-bottomed holes in wood, used in

1. Countersunk bit,
2. Twist drill bit,
3. Dowel bit,
4. Masonry drill bit, 5. Spade bit,
6. Auger bit.

either hand or power drills.

Auger bit This is for making holes above 6.5mm (¼in) in wood.

Spade bit Used for the same job as the auger bit but with a power drill.

Countersink bit This is used for chamfering the edge of a hole for a countersunk-head screw so that the head sits flush with the surface of the wood.

Combination drill bit This can be used to drill both a pilot hole and a countersunk edge for woodscrews in one action.

Plugging bit This drills out a matching plug from a similar piece of timber to cover and conceal a screw head.

Masonry bit This has a special, hard tip, designed to drill into brick walls. Use the masonry bit with an electric hammer action drill for concrete surfaces.

1. Pistol-grip hand drill, *2. Hand brace,* *3. Cordless drill,* *4. Hand drill,* *5. Electric drill,*
6. Bradawl, *7. Gimlet,* *8. Chuck key.*

FIXING TO WALLS

A nail usually bends when hammered into a brick wall, and a screw either will not go in at all or, if it does, will not grip well enough to serve the purpose. The method you use to fix things to walls depends on the type of wall you are dealing with.

All that is needed in a solid wall is a wallplug that expands as the screw is driven home to hold it fast.

However, this is of no use in a hollow wall of plasterboard or lath and plaster where either the screw positions have to be placed where the studs fall or a special hollow-wall fastener with an anchor or toggle holds the screw in position by tightening up against the back of the plasterboard. The latter is not suitable for heavy loads.

Masonry walls

These are solid walls constructed from bricks or building blocks.

On a solid wall a wallplug, usually of plastic, is used to hold the screw securely in the wall. Some will take special screws which are hammered in. It is important to use a plug size that matches the screw size. The plug should fit the hole tightly enough to need pushing in with your thumb or lightly tapping home with a hammer. When a wood screw is screwed into the plug the plug expands and tightly grips the sides of the hole. The depth of hole should match the plug, not the screw.

Extruded plugs These are straight-sided plugs which need to be used with some care. They come in long lengths and you cut off the amount required. The whole length of the plug should be sunk into the masonry, rather than left flush with the plaster surface, as otherwise the plaster may crack when the screw is driven home. Also, the shank of the screw should not go into the plug, only the thread, or the tight fit may cause the screw to snap.

Moulded wallplugs These tapering plugs are easier to use as most are shaped to take the screw shank and part of a countersunk screw head. They do not need to be pushed right to the end of a hole and many have a lip that stops them going in too far.

Hollow walls

These are usually interior walls and are made of skim plastered plasterboard or, in older houses, lath and plaster. The surface material is nailed to vertical timbers (studs).

For a strong fixing it is important to screw into these studs. In this case no plug is needed as wood screws can

be screwed directly into the studs.

To find the positions of the studs, which are usually at 400mm (16in) intervals, first knock the wall with a screwdriver. The studs, when hit, will sound more solid. Then push a bradawl into the wall to check (see also Safety Tip).

If you want to fix a light object to a hollow wall you can use a specially designed plug usually called a toggle or anchor. A special wallplug may be suitable for a narrow cavity of 10mm (⅜in) but most of these fittings will need a cavity of 25–30mm (1–1¼in) and some may need more than 50mm (2in). Anchors cope best with thinner board, most being suitable for 3–12mm (⅛in–½in), some for up to 20mm (¾in). Most toggles will cope with thicker boards, some up to 75mm (3in).

Anchors and toggles

Special wallplug Wings at the side expand to grip the back of the panel when the screw is put into it. This type of plug remains in place if the screw is removed.

Plastic toggle The anchor is squeezed through the hole and spreads out to grip the back of the board as the screw is tightened.

Gravity toggle A bolt sits against the screw to be pushed through the hole then drops down to fit against the board back when the screw is tightened. It is lost on removal.

Spring toggle A butterfly type bolt fits around the screw to slot through the hole then opens out behind the board. It is lost on removal.

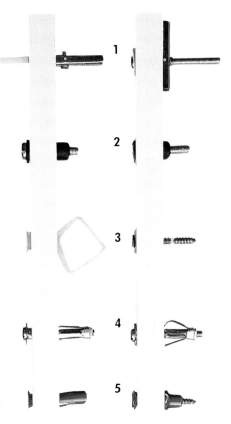

1. Gravity toggle, 2. Rubber fixing, 3, 4 and 5 Plastic and metal anchors.

PLANES AND SURFORMS

Designed for removing unwanted portions of wood and reducing timber to size, plus shaping it and leaving it smooth and flat, planes need to be kept sharp. The edge should be parallel with, and just protruding from, the base plate when in use. The longer the piece of wood to be worked on, the longer the plane should be so that it levels out the length rather than following the wood's profile.

Types of plane

Bench plane This is designed for smoothing edges of wood with the grain and comes in a number of sizes. The one with the longest sole plate, a jointer plane, is just under 600mm (23in) long, a jack plane is 350–375mm (14–15in) and a smoothing plane is 200–300mm (8–9in).

Block plane Smaller than a bench plane, a block plane is useful for working on small pieces of timber, for smoothing end grain and for trimming plastic laminates. It has a sole plate of 140–180mm (5½–7in) and can be used with one hand, although two hands are usually used when trimming end grain.

Replaceable-blade plane This can be used with a number of different types of blade and is a good choice for people who do not have sharpening equipment. It can be used in the same way as a bench plane, and is usually slightly longer and narrower than a smoothing plane.

Surform This tool does not give the same smooth finish as a plane but it is a quick and easy way to remove material from wood plus soft metals, plastics and laminates.

Power planer If you do a lot of planing this takes the hard work out of the job. They also cut rebates.

Special purpose planes There are also planes for making rebates, for cutting grooves, for cleaning tenons and for planing curves.

Sharpening planes

New planes need to be sharpened and all planes should be checked before they are used. You will require a medium or fine oilstone which you should keep in a box with sides slightly shallower than the stone to allow the blade to run off the stone edge. Use oil or paraffin on the stone and wipe with a soft cloth or kitchen roll frequently to keep clean.

A blade has a grinding angle of

1. Smoothing plane, **2 and 3**. Surforms, **4**. Jack plane, **5**. Replaceable-blade plane, **6**. Power planer.

25° and a sharpening or honing angle of 30° (increase to 38° when planing manmade boards). New blades come with the 25° bevel on the front edge but need sharpening. Use a honing guide to help you maintain the correct angle and rub the blade, bevel side down, backwards and forwards along the length of the stone until a burr of metal builds up along the edge. Then reverse the blade, laying it flat on the stone, and rub backwards and forwards a few times to remove the burr or bend it back. Check the sharpness on paper; when sharp it will make a clean cut.

Using planes

Planing long lengths of wood When planing along the grain of a length of wood apply slightly more pressure at the front of the plane as you start, then even downward pressure along the length. At the end, apply pressure at the back of the plane. Each stroke should be the whole length of the wood.

Planing edges When planing long edges with a bench plane hold the plane down with the thumb of your second hand and use your fingers as a guide along the side. Always work along the grain.

On a short edge When using a block plane work from each edge towards the centre, again using your fingers as a guide.

SANDING, ADHESIVES AND FILLERS

For smoothing surfaces sanding papers and sanders are ideal. There are a number of different types of sanding paper, some suitable for specific materials, some more long lasting than others. A sanding block makes working on flat surfaces easier and a sanding attachment for an electric drill, takes the hard work out of some jobs but is not as powerful as a specially designed sander.

Choosing an adhesive will depend on the size of the job, what material is being glued to the timber and whether it will be in use indoors or outside.

As wood constantly expands and contracts fillers must be able to cope with this, particularly outdoors, where conditions are most extreme.

Abrasive papers

These are mainly sold in sheets with the grade or grit size marked on the back. There are three common grades, coarse, medium and fine, but others are also available. Abrasive papers also come in shapes to fit power sanders and drill attachments. On a surface in poor condition start with a coarse grade and finish with the fines one.

Glasspaper Wears quickly but inexpensive.

Garnet paper Ideal for finishing wood.

Wet or dry paper Used wet to rub down painted surfaces. It can also be used to clean metals.

Emery Used mainly for cleaning or polishing metal.

Tungsten carbide Long lasting and hard abrasive.

Sanding block Abrasive paper can be wrapped around a block of cork or wood to make sanding flat surfaces easier and more accurate.

Power sanders

Sanding attachments for electric drill. Circular sanding discs are used over a rubber backing pad to sand wood, plastic or metal but they produce wave type marks. They are most suitable for removing old paint. The alternative is a flap wheel sander which has a slower, gentler action and does not produce the marks.

Orbital sander A strip of abrasive paper is slotted on to the base and moves at high speed in a series of orbits to provide a smooth finish

Belt sander These are ideal for sanding floors. Usually fitted with a dust collection bag, they are large, powerful sanders that need two hands and are usually hired.

1. Flap wheel sander attachment, 2. Plastic wood in tube, 3. Wood stopping, 4. Plastic wood in tin, 5. PVA adhesive, 6. Waterproof PVA, **7 and 8**. Alternative PVA adhesives.

Adhesives

In most cases, when working with wood, you can use a PVA (polyvinyl acetate) adhesive especially designed for sticking timber. This will bond wood to wood and wood to many other materials. Wipe surplus glue away with a wet rag before it sets. Where the joint might get hot or cold or be subjected to moisture, it is important to use one sold for outdoor purposes.

PVA is also suitable for use when adding a veneer but if you are fitting a plastic laminate to wood – a kitchen or bathroom worktop for instance – you should use a contact adhesive. Some of these allow some movement before the glue sets so you can get a perfect match, others set instantly on contact so are more difficult to use in this case.

Fillers

Outdoor cracks between wood and brickwork Gaps around doors and windows should be filled during dry weather. Mastic fillers are available for deep cracks of this sort. Pack very deep gaps first with newspaper, leaving a gap of 10–15mm (⅜–⅝in) for the filler.

Cracks in wood joints In this sort of gap, in window frames for example, again use a mastic outdoors. Indoors use a general purpose filler that allows for some movement.

Holes and cracks in unpainted wood For small holes and cracks in unpainted wood use wood stopping. This comes in different shades to match different timbers. Apply with a knife until just proud of the surface then leave to dry, which will not take long. When dry, sand flush with the surface. You may have to apply two layers to fill a large hole.

TIMBER

The very many different species of trees break down, as far as woodworking is concered, into two groups: hardwoods and softwoods. Hardwoods come from broadleafed deciduous trees like oak, beech and ash, softwoods come from coniferous evergreens such as spruce, pine and cedar.

Hardwoods are considered more durable, are more expensive and are more difficult to work with. Used mainly for furniture, hardwoods are usually stained and polished or varnished to show off their decorative grains. Because of their cost hardwoods are not used a lot in do-it-yourself work, manmade boards with a thin veneer of hardwood being more common.

Softwoods are much cheaper than hardwoods and are easier to work. They are used in the construction of houses for joists, rafters, flooring, window frames and doors, staircases plus partitions and for some furniture. Exposed softwoods are painted or varnished.

Buying softwoods

Softwoods are available sawn as well as planed all round. Sawn timber is cut with power saws to standard widths and thicknesses. The stated sizes in both cases are those as cut from the log. Because timber shrinks as it dries the size when you buy it is often slightly less than the stated size.

Softwoods used outdoors need protecting with preservative or paint. Some timber is available which has been pressure impregnated with preservative. In this case only cut ends will need additional treatment.

Softwoods

Douglas fir Considered one of the best softwoods available, it can be finished by staining and polishing. It is used for flooring, furniture, window frames and in structural work.
Parana pine Available in long, wide boards often without knots. During drying it shrinks and twists rapidly, so select straight boards and use immediately.
Redwood Commonly known as deal, this is the most widely available softwood. It is easy to work and can be painted, stained or varnished.
Whitewood This is in fact spruce. It has a straight grain and fine texture, is easy to work provided it is dry and can be painted, stained and varnished satisfactorily. It is used indoors only, for a veneer for plywood and for furniture, joinery and flooring.

Buying hardwoods

Hardwoods, apart from being more expensive, are also more difficult to buy than softwoods and the range of sizes is usually smaller.

Tools need to be sharp but hardwoods provide a better result than softwoods when turned or jointed and is often used for mouldings.

Hardwood is sold planed all round (PAR). This is timber that has been sawn then had its sides smoothed and made parallel by planing.

Increasingly popular as an alternative to traditional hardwood is the range of veneered and faced boards now available. Take care when you purchase this material that the sheets are completely flat – they are extremely hard to straighten once they become distorted.

Hardwoods and veneers

Ash This is a beautiful pale colour and is mainly for furniture, especially where the wood has to be bent.
Beech This is also light in colour with a straight grain. It is good for turning and so is popular for chairs and children's toys.
Iroko This is similar to teak but is less expensive. It is used for garden furniture as it is very durable.
Mahogany This has a warm red colour, is strong, easy to work and can be used outside if preservative treated. Widely used for furniture, mahogany is now more commonly seen as a veneer on chipboard or on a plank.
Oak-faced blockboard A very durable veneer in which the decorative face is generally on one side only.

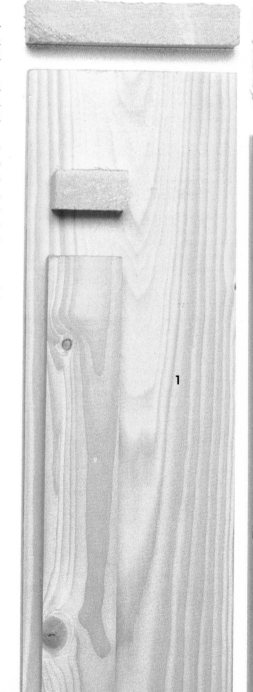

1 and 2. PAR (planed all round) softwood, 3. Sawn softwood, 4. Preservative-impregnated sawn softwood.

Birch-faced blockboard This is an extremely strong material which should be used with its wood-strip core lengthways. The wood veneer generally covers the core on both sides.

Checking for faults

Wood comes in a range of qualities. The better the quality the fewer faults should be present. Constructional softwood is of a less high grade than joinery softwood; the latter should be used where the wood will be on show.

Knots Avoid large or dead knots (those with a bark ring around them) as they weaken the timber and can fall out. Small live knots (those without an outer bark ring) will not affect the strength and can add to the decorative effect of the timber. If you paint the timber, coat all knots with knotting first.

Cracks These are known as checks (splits along the length) or shakes (cracks across the grain). Apart from obvious splits or cracks, also avoid those which follow the curve of the growth rings (cup shakes). End shakes or cup shakes that are near a corner are acceptable.

Waney edge This is when bark and sapwood are left on the timber to provide maximum width. These should be removed.

MANMADE BOARD

Manmade board is, in most cases, cheaper than timber, has good resistance to warping and comes in much larger widths. It is, however, not usually suitable for use outside. The choice of finishes is wide, from hardwood and softwood veneers to melamine in white and a range of colours. Hardboard also comes with a tiled finish and in perforated patterns. Boards should be stored flat to avoid buckling and can be satisfactorily worked using standard woodworking tools.

Chipboard

This is made from flake-sized particles of timber coated with resin and then pressed under heat and pressure. It is available in a number of stock sizes from 1220 × 2400mm (4ft × 8ft) to 1830 × 3680mm (6ft × 12ft) and most common thicknesses are 12mm (½in), 18mm (¾in) and 25mm (1in).

Plain chipboard comes in three main grades: standard grade, which has smooth surfaces ready for painting and is used for making furniture and construction work; flooring grade, which can be used instead of a timber floor; and moisture-resistant, suitable for use in a damp atmosphere, but not outdoors.

Blockboard

This is made up of a core of softwood strips, glued together all at the same angle, and faced with veneer on each side. Blockboard can be used for table tops, worktops, doors, furniture and wide shelves.

Laminboard

This is similar to blockboard and used for the same functions but it is more expensive and heavier. The strips are a mixture of soft- and hardwoods with a smoother finish.

Pineboard

This is another laminated board but is made up of strips of pine edge-glued together. Its use is the same as for blockboard and laminboard.

Plywood

This is made of thin sheets of wood glued together, the direction of the grain alternating strip by strip. The number of plies varies according to the thickness, but the thickness of the layers can also vary. There are grades for indoors or out with a range of uses from shelving and furniture to building material.

Hardboard

This is made from pulped timber hot-pressed into thin sheets. There is a wide range of finishes available. The standard type with one smooth and one rough surface can be used to provide an even base on floors for an overlay of vinyl tiles or sheet flooring and for drawer bases and backs when making fitted furniture.

Oil-tempered hardboard is water-resistant and can be used outside. There is also mediumboard which comes as HM (high density) and LM (low density); this is used for lining walls, ceilings and partitions. Duofaced has the fine sealed surface on both sides.

Pegboard has holes or slots punched in it, sometimes in patterns, and this can be used for decorative grilles. Hardboard also provides the backing for tile-look, embossed, patterned or wood grain finishes, and for melamine.

Medium density fibreboard

Like hardboard, MDF is made from wood fibres bonded together under pressure but the bonding agent used makes it exceptionally strong. It can be machined to different profiles and so can be used as a substitute for timber moulding and panelling.

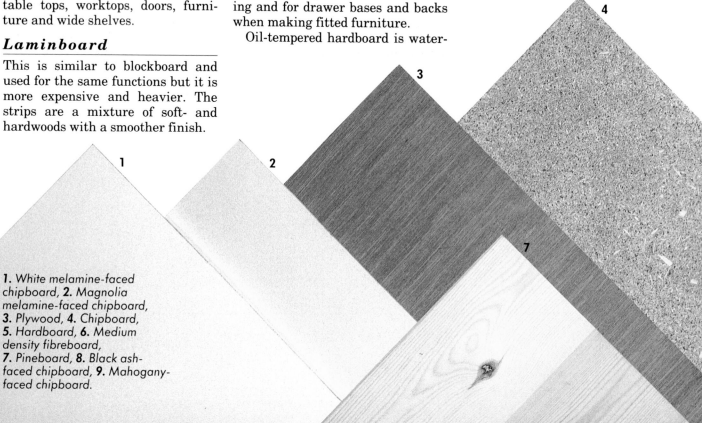

1. *White melamine-faced chipboard,* 2. *Magnolia melamine-faced chipboard,* 3. *Plywood,* 4. *Chipboard,* 5. *Hardboard,* 6. *Medium density fibreboard,* 7. *Pineboard,* 8. *Black ash-faced chipboard,* 9. *Mahogany-faced chipboard.*

Using chipboard

Chipboard can be sawn in the normal way but tools blunt more quickly than with use on other materials. Score the surfaces of faced chipboard before sawing as this will help to stop chipping, or use circular saw blades designed for the purpose.

Chipboard cannot be successfully screwed or nailed close to the edge. Either attach an edge of solid wood to the board into which attachments can be screwed or use special joint blocks. Special chipboard screws are easier to handle and provide more grip than standard ones; chipboard can also be glued.

Finish edges with special edging strip or use a strip of timber. Standard chipboard can be painted or polyurethane varnished, or stained and varnished. Wood veneer chipboard can be polyurethane varnished or polished.

Using blockboard, laminboard or pineboard

This can be cut in the usual way. Where possible, cut with the length running in the same direction as the core strips and take care with the ends as this material tends to split.

This type of board can be screwed and glued successfully along the length but not along edges where the cut is across the grain.

Paint, varnish or plastic laminate can all be used on blockboard. You can glue or pin on timber strip for edging. Pineboard can be varnished or polished.

Using plywood

To prevent chipping the surface veneers, score both sides before cutting. Use a tenon saw on thin plywoods up to 6mm (¼in); thicker ones should be cut with a panel or power saw. Cut through from the decorative surface (that means with the backing uppermost when using a jigsaw as this cuts on the up stroke).

Plywood takes nails, pins, screws and glue well. To prevent surface damage, drill pilot holes for screws and pins. When gluing, roughen surfaces to provide a good key and try to make sure that the grain on both pieces runs in the same direction.

You can fill and paint the edges or finish them with metal or plastic stripping or timber. All are best glued in place. Paint, stain or varnish the surfaces but finish both surfaces in the same way.

Using hardboard

Like most manmade board, hardboard should normally be stored flat. However, before fixing, stand the sheets separately on edge where they are to be used for periods as follows: standard board 72 hours, medium board 48 hours, tempered hardboard 5 days. If you want to use hardboard in a damp atmosphere such as a kitchen or bathroom you should wash it from the mesh side with a litre of water for each 2400mm × 1220mm (8ft × 4ft) sheet then lay it flat, with sheets back to back, for the following periods; standard board 48 hours, tempered board 72 hours.

Cut hardboard with a tenon saw from the smooth side. Score the surface of painted or laminated hardboard and cut to the waste side. Plane and rub down the edges.

Where possible, use special hardboard pins to fix. Hardboard can be glued from either side; roughen the smooth side first to provide a key. It can be painted or wallpapered.

Using MDF

Medium density fibreboard can be cut with a panel or power saw and, unlike other types of board except pineboard, it can also be shaped with a plane or chisel. Place scrap timber behind the board when drilling.

Fix in the same way as for chipboard. The smooth finish means that little preparation work, apart from a light sanding, is needed before painting or staining and varnishing.

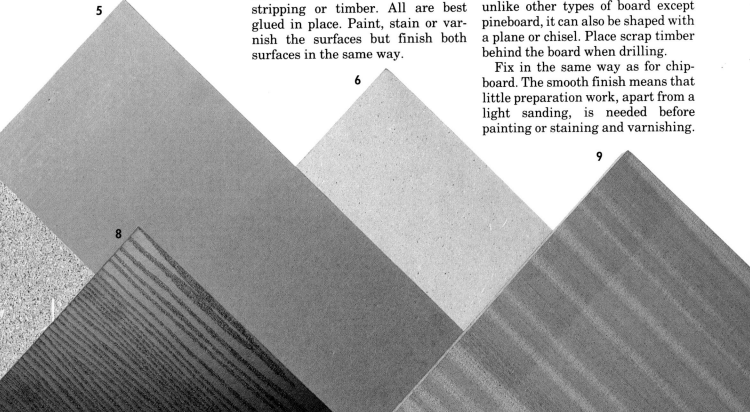

MOULDINGS

There is a wide range of mouldings available in both softwood and hardwood and a smaller range of vinyl made to look like timber. You can use moulding to hide a join, to retain glass in a door and for other specific purposes or just for decoration. Designs can be simple or intricate and it is possible to get old mouldings copied or to find them in architectural salvage yards if you want to match up an original design. Small-size mouldings come in standard lengths of 2m (6ft 6in) and 3m (9ft 9in). Larger mouldings are usually sold, like timber, in lengths.

Choosing mouldings

Architrave This is used to finish off the join between a door frame, a window frame or a fitted cupboard and the adjoining wall.

Astragal A decorative shape half-round moulding, this is normally used to cover a joint.

Corner This L-shaped moulding is used to finish off a corner where two boards join or as lipping to cover the edge of a shelf or worktop.

Corner pieces These are individual decorative shapes that can be inserted at the corners where two lengths of moulding meet.

Cornice Usually of softwood, this can be used instead of polystyrene or plaster coving to cover the join between wall and ceiling.

Dado rail This is used for decoration part way up the wall, usually about 91cm (36in) above the floor.

Dowel This is a completely round moulding that in its smaller diameters is used for making joints. Larger sizes are used for curtain poles, towel rails or broom handles.

Edge nosing A moulding with a groove and a curved edge, this is used to fit over shelf or stair edges.

Half-round This can be used to cover the join between two butting panels or manmade boards.

Picture rail This moulding was originally intended to carry pictures, but is now mainly decorative.

Quadrant This quarter-dowel moulding is used for covering internal corners such as that between floor and built-in furniture. Smaller sizes may be used as glazing beads.

Scotia Used in the same situations as quadrant, the curve is concave as compared with quadrant's convex shape. Larger shapes are also used in place of cornice.

Skirting A cover for the gap where wall meets floor.

Square and rectangular These are very simple and can be used for shelf or board edgings.

Triangular This moulding is an alternative to quadrant or scotia for internal corners but is traditionally used as stair rods.

Fixing mouldings

The method you choose to fix a moulding depends on the weight of the moulding and the type of surface you are fixing it to. Heavy skirting is fixed with flat brads or screws; architrave and dado rails can be screwed or nailed and glued in place. Most lighter mouldings can be pinned and glued to wooden or plaster surfaces. Always use oval wire nails so you do not split the wood. Knock nail heads home with a nail punch and fill with wood filler.

1. *Moulded skirting,* 2. *Decorative architrave,* 3. *Dado,* 4. *Plain architrave,* 5. *Corner moulding,* 6. *Scotia,* 7. *Half-round moulding,* 8. *Square-edge moulding,* 9. *Edge moulding,* 10. *Quadrant,* 11. *Astragal,* 12. *Dowel.*

DOORS, KNOBS AND HANDLES

The range of internal doors, both for rooms and for cupboards, allows you to pick a design that fits in with the period of the house and with the surrounding decor. Some come ready finished, others can be stained, painted or decorated in a variety of ways for an individual look. Door knobs, lever latch and pull handles come in many sizes and a choice of modern and traditional designs and finishes.

Panelled interior door

Traditional-design interior doors are widely available in pine, hardwood and, newer and cheaper, pressed fibre. The timber ones usually come ready varnished. Panelled doors lend themselves to mirror tiling and to decorative paint treatments like dragging or tortoiseshelling.

Flush door

This is the cheapest type of interior door and comes white-painted or wood-veneered. Both flush and panelled room doors can be used for cupboards too.

Glazed interior door

This usually comes with small glazing panels that can be used for clear or obscure glass.

Cupboard doors

Panelled Pine and hardwood door panels come in a huge range of widths and heights suitable for use for bedroom, living or kitchen storage and include drawer fronts.
Louvres Louvred panels come unfinished in the same sort of range of widths and heights as panelled ones. They can be varnished, stained and sealed or painted.

Knobs and handles

Traditional brass knobs Plain round brass knobs and ornate rope and octagonal designs come in a wide range of sizes.
China knobs Available in white, gold edged or with a floral design.
Plastic knobs Available in bright colours and pastel shades. All these are available for doors, as well as furniture.
Wood knobs Can be stained to match the furniture.
Lever latches For room doors there are traditional design brass lever latches, some with china handles.
Pull handles These come in a range from traditional brass to modern, brightly coloured plastic. They are often known as D-handles.
Drop and rebate handles Suitable for drawers. Available in plain and more ornate traditional designs.

Left: 1. Hardwood panel door, **2 and 3.** Louvre doors, **4.** Softwood panel door, **5 and 6.** Sliding cupboard doors.

Right: Top row, door knobs; the other handles are all suitable for different styles of cupboards and drawers.

PROTECTION AND FINISHES

Stains are used to tint the surface of wood and varnishes serve to protect it. They are always used on bare wood to show off the grain and give a transparent or semi-transparent coating. Stain colours will be affected by the natural colour of the wood and by its rate of absorption, so it is wise to do a test on a scrap of the same timber first.

Clear varnish will change the colour slightly. To check the varnished colour, damp the wood and this will give you an idea of the effect. Preservatives are used to protect wood outside and oils and wax polishes give interior wood a soft sheen.

Indoors

Linseed oil Provides a finish that is water-resistant. It can become slightly sticky in time and this stickiness will attract dirt and dust.

Wax polish For a longer lasting finish, seal the surface first with shellac sanding sealer or similar product before applying the wax polish.

Transparent polyurethane varnish This provides a tough finish for floors, stripped doors, shelves and panelling.

Stains To change the colour of wood, use a stain. Stains can be water-based or oil-based; the latter kind are the easier to use. After staining, you will need to apply a protective finish of polish or varnish compatible with the stain.

Stained varnish In these the stain is contained within the varnish and this is applied with a brush.

Outside

Varnish Usually sold as yacht varnish, there are special tough, clear varnishes especially suitable for outdoor use on garden furniture.

Teak oil Apply two coats of teak oil across the grain. Suitable for use indoors or outside.

Microporous paint This is designed for use on exterior woodwork which has not been painted. It allows wood to breathe but still gives it protection.

Stained preservative For use on rough or smooth exterior timber, there are two main types – solvent- and water-based. Solvent-based preservatives also stop wood fading and include a fungicide. They can be harmful to plants and wildlife while wet. Water-based preservatives come in a smaller range of colours, are not so long-lasting and are not harmful. Creosote is the traditional preservative for fences; this is tar-based and can damage plants.

Above: A selection of stains and finishes for interior and exterior woodwork.

HINGES AND HOOKS

There is a hinge to suit practically every situation. For room doors there are tough butt hinges and rising butt hinges designed so that the door rises as it opens to go over carpet. One hinge allows a door to fold back flat against the wall, another allows two doors to swing on the same hinge. Some are designed for surface-mounted cupboard doors, some are self-shutting.

Hooks come in many finishes and many sizes from minute to large L-shaped hooks that store ladders, bicycles, spare timber and other large objects off the floor.

Hinges

Butt hinge Comes in a wide range of sizes and brass-plated, steel or zinc.

Rising butt hinge Designed so that the door rises slightly as it opens, allowing it to clear thick floor coverings.

Parliament hinge For use where the door is to fold back flat against the wall.

Double-door hinge Allows two doors to be hung side by side from the same frame.

Flush hinge Suitable for light cupboard doors.

Concealed hinge For use on lay-on doors. Some are also self-closing.

Continuous hinge This is cut to the length required and is used mainly on chest and cabinet lids.

Table flap hinge For use on a fold-down worktop or table, this provides a flush joint in both raised and lowered positions.

Hooks

Screw-in hook Often called a cup hook, this hook screws into timber.

Coat hook Available in brass or chrome finish, this can be screwed to a batten to make a coat rack or to the back of a solid or panelled door.

Flush door hook With small pins attached that are lightly hammered into the door, these can take insubstantial items only.

Self-adhesive hook With a self-adhesive backing, this plastic hook comes in white or colours and can be simply stuck to tiles or a flush door. It will only take light items.

Giant hook This L-shaped hook comes in a range of sizes to hold items from small DIY tools to bicycles and ladders.

Tool clip This comes in sizes from 13mm–38mm (½in–1½in) to clasp a range of tool handles.

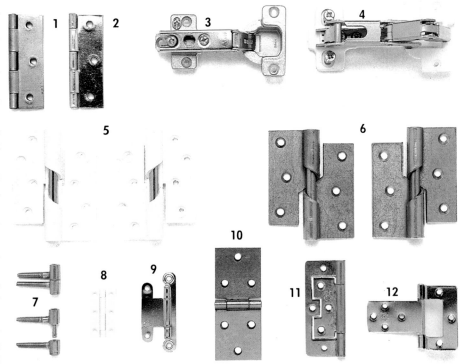

Above: 1 and 2. Butt hinges in two finishes, 3 and 4. Concealed hinges, 5. Nylon rising butt hinges, 6. Steel rising butt hinges, 7. Pivot hinges, 8. Small nylon butt hinge, 9. Flat semi-concealed hinge, 10. Back flap, 11 and 12. Flush hinges

Below: 1. Bicycle hook, 2, 3 and 4. Coat hooks, 5. Bill clip, 6. Double hook, 7. Brass cup hooks, 8 and 9. Large hooks for tools, 10. Self-adhesive hooks, 11. Tea-towel hook, 12. Plastic-coated cup hooks.

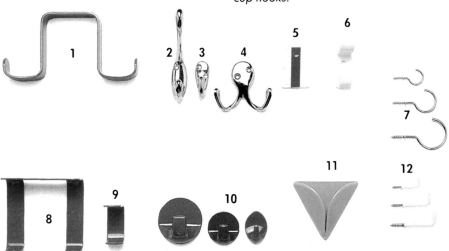

INDEX

96

The publishers would like to thank the following organisations and individuals for their kind permission to reproduce the photographs in this book:
Acmetrack Ltd: title page, 52, 54 above and centre.
Camera Press Limited: 8, 9 above, 17 below, 23 top left, 28 below, 30, 31, 32, 33, 34.
Dialene: 29.
ELFA Domestic Storage Systems Ltd: 3, 54 bottom.
H Plan: 26–7.
C Richardson: 44.
STC Telecommunications: 15 right.
Jessica Strang: 11 above, 16 right, 19, 21 bottom left, 23 bottom right, 30 left.

Elizabeth Whiting & Associates: 21 below, /Michael Crockett (Jarvis Woolgar) 9 below, /Michael Dunne (Patricia Sayad) 12 above, /Clive Helm 15 left, /Rodney Hyett 22, /David Lloyd 13, /Neil Lorimer 23 below, 24 above, /Michael Nicholson (Derek Walker) 23 centre, /Spike Powell (Caroline MacDonald) 20, (Barbara Palmer) 21 above, /Ron Sutherland 14, 18, / Friedhelm Thomas 6, 64, /Jerry Tubby (Babcock) 17 above, (Lila Corbett) 12 below.
World Press Network Ltd: 10 above, 16 left.

All subjects for special photography supplied by Sainsbury's Homebase.